Namesake

NAMESAKE

MICHEL GOLDBERG

YALE UNIVERSITY PRESS

NEW HAVEN AND LONDON

This book was previously published in 1980
in France by Hachette as *Ecorché Juif*.

Designed by Sally Harris
and set in Garamond type.
Printed in the United States of America by
Vail-Ballou Press, Binghamton, N.Y.

Library of Congress Cataloging in Publication Data

Goldberg, Michel, 1938-
  Namesake.

  Translation of: Ecorché juif.
  1. Goldberg, Michel, 1938-   . 2. Jews—France—
Biography. 3. Children of Holocaust survivors—France—
Biography. 4. Entebbe Airport Raid, 1976—Personal
narratives. 5. France—Ethnic relations. I. Title.
DS135.F9G6413   944'.004924024   82-50443
ISBN 0-300-02790-7   AACR2

10 9 8 7 6 5 4 3 2 1

A celle qui viendra

CONTENTS

ACKNOWLEDGMENTS

I wish to express my gratitude to those who helped me live through this adventure, in particular Ron and Marie-José; to those who remained at my side during the delivery of this book, my children, my adoptive father, Biquette, Gabriella, Zwi, Manfred, Jean and Michelle, Ilione, Yvonne, and Doris; and to those who helped to get it translated and published in English, Ivar and Gladys.

In a category of her own, I thank my mother, who gave me life several times and loved me the only way she could.

They and others will be happy to know that with the writing of this book the pain in my right hand disappeared.

This book is largely autobiographical. Still, some liberties with the facts have been taken to protect people or institutions I care for, or to spare the reader some unnecessary meanders. All public events, in particular the Barbie affair and the Entebbe incident, are described as faithfully as possible.

The key to your adventures is the guilt feeling that forced you to pay for imaginary sins over and over again.

—Arthur Koestler, *Arrival and Departure*

CHAPTER 0 *False Start*

And now Barbie is there, at my mercy. Rather elegant in his brown suit, his back turned to me, he stands much closer than the watermelons I used for target practice. There are very few people around, and even if one of my bullets should go through him, the risk of harming anyone else is practically nil.

I am very calm. The revolver rests lightly on my lap, under the poncho, my hand on the grip and cylinder. I feel no pity, even having met him.

That he has his back to me doesn't bother me. It is no more courageous to shoot an unarmed man from the front than from behind. And besides, I can always call out to him or step down from the curb. I would be on him in two strides.

Will.

All I need is the will.

PART I

Sweet France

Douce France
Cher pays de mon enfance
Bercé de tendre insouciance . . .

—Charles Trenet

CHAPTER 1 *Stillborn Identity*

Berthe Dreyfuss, my mother's mother, was from Lorraine and anti-Semitic. She made no attempt to hide the fact that she was Jewish—Dreyfuss!—but anti-Semitic she was. Descended in a direct line from the Prophets, she would detour by Rumplemeyer's, the chic Alsatian confectioner in Paris, to avoid the herring-eaters from the banks of the Vistula, the tailors from the Carpathians, the furriers from the Danube—in short, the whole Yiddish world, which she would have considered out of place in her salon. To be accepted by her, a Jew had to be famous or dead; or else free of any sign of a "Jewish" nose, accent, or trade and able to extend his little finger properly as he sipped his Darjeeling.

My grandmother was one of those "of Jewish origin"— a few more syllables between them and the Temple—who claimed at least spiritual kinship with Heine, Bergson, Mendelssohn, and even that Sephardi, Spinoza. Her parents had chosen exile in Montmartre because they wanted to remain French after the Prussians snatched Alsace-Lorraine. She thus became a colleague of Joan of Arc, flaunting her Lorraineness and demanding revenge as she nibbled petits fours.

Separation between Church and State at the turn of the century enabled French Jews to put aside the substance of their Judaism and to savor roast pork in the name of free thought. Soon the sons of Jacob thought of themselves as Jacobins. The illusion lasted until others, declaring themselves to be "real" Frenchmen—even though, from Coblenz to Sigmaringen, they usually stood on the wrong side of the Rhine—banned them from public parks and drinking establishments. It is to the Nazis and even more to the Vichyites that French Jews owe their renewed sense of identity. No doubt we should be grateful to them. But I am getting ahead of my story.

Between the epidemic of Spanish flu and General Nivelle's short-lived attacks on the Aisne in 1917, Berthe Dreyfuss gave birth to her second child, another girl and redheaded to boot: my mother. You might call her a war accident. Faint shadow of her older sister, and soon followed by a son-Messiah, she counted for so little that her mother sometimes said in an élan of sadism, "I should have aborted you." This missed miscarriage led my mother to approach life with vertigo. She feared both life and death, the present and the future, herself as well as others. She strove for perfection as a penance for having come into the world uninvited. Always the best behaved, engrossed in her homework, she deprived herself of childhood in the hope of pleasing her parents. The more she strove the less she succeeded. Unwelcome to the world, she could only perpetuate the curse that I am trying to break today: the inability to love.

She got even with my grandmother by marrying a Polish Jewish tailor. Then came my turn. I first saw the night in Paris in November 1938—it was Kristallnacht.

What memories I have of my father, Joseph Goldberg, are a mixture of the stories I have been told and what I imagine. The words one puts into the mouths of the dead! One cold February morning he disappeared from my childhood without trace or date. He had wanted me to go with him to Lyon, that Monday, for a breath of fresh air—which was excellent where we were—and no doubt for one of those moments of father-son complicity. But there was snow on the ground and my boots were being mended. My mother's fear that I might catch my death of cold saved my life. That is how I happen to dream even today that my arm is tattooed with six bluish-black numbers, now enormous since they have expanded as I have grown.

I was not deported and so only I can free myself of the burden of not having accompanied my father.

On the way to Auschwitz, he stopped over at Beaune-la-Rolande, a little town in the Loiret thus saved from nothingness. My mother tried to help him escape by bribing a French guard with a bolt of fabric that she had rescued from the debacle. She failed, but didn't dare ask the guard to return the fabric. She was not in a good bargaining position, and times were hard for guards too.

My father had come to Lyon with two identity cards: a false one, which he had just acquired, and a real one, which he intended to give to a foreign Jew. For Vichy, in its zeal to please the Germans, had on its own segmented France's Jewish population according to the best marketing principles; and for a little while French Jews harbored the illusion that they would be treated better than stateless ones and nationals from the occupied countries to the east. So delighted was my father with his French naturalization that he thought it must surely have some value. For a long time I was ashamed that he had believed in this grim distinction. I was especially ashamed that he did not seek ordination into the Resistance, at the risk of death with a gun in his hand or even deportation. I had to be content with a father who had behaved only a little better than most Frenchmen. He, like the rest of his unit, was "present and ready for combat at the eight o'clock roll call on June 27, 1940," after a retreat of almost 250 miles, which General Frère's dispatch blushingly referred to as a withdrawal, "in order to avoid the disgrace of surrender in open country."

My mother was promoted to head of a family of two. A woman at bay, frightened of everything, she was in her element. She saved the life she had given me at least ten times. I was the only person who could not harm her; my weakness was her strength. Since her own mother had begrudged her food, she measured her quality as a mother by the quantity of it she was able to force into me. It didn't matter that food was rationed and expensive. It would be all the more to her credit to display constant ingenuity, patience, and energy in finding a little ham or flounder for her child. It didn't matter whether or not I was hungry. She would brandish a burning newspaper over my head or threaten to scald me until I opened my mouth, into which she would quickly thrust the lifesaving spoon. Her own mother's bosom had been cold, her kisses infrequent pecks, so my mother devoured me with kisses—but devoured I was.

Sometimes we had to leave home at night and get into a wood-fueled truck or catch an elusive train. I still remember a meal in a dining car where we were seated with two German soldiers, one of whom offered me a piece of candy, thus discharging his instructions to be "korrect." My mother and I finally settled in a pretty little village on the outskirts of Normandy, where she hoped to find butter and no guns. She was only half mistaken.

I had no idea that I was Jewish. It was prudent for me not to know, in case I was questioned. I didn't even know what a Jew was. It didn't bother me to have two different names, neither of which was mine. I was Parisian by birth, but I had to pretend to be a native first of Fourmies, in the north, because the town hall had been bombed and all its records destroyed—or so we hoped—then of Blida, because Algeria was, at the time, more French than France and it was impossible to obtain a birth certificate from there.

After much hesitation, my mother took a chance and enrolled me in the village school. As long as she was lying about my name and my place of birth, she also lied about my age, "to put me ahead." Such were the beginnings of my career as a model student. I was almost always at the top of my class and probably bathed more frequently than my fellows.

In season, I would go into the nearby woods in the morning and gather mushrooms, one of the rare items that the Germans had not succeeded in rationing. How proud I was to come home, before leaving for school, with my basket half full of coulemelles and rosés des prés. My mother would be ecstatic. She could exchange them for eggs or cream—gold, so to speak.

When I was old enough, my mother sent me to church like the other children, so as not to arouse suspicion. Mass was a little boring, but our suppressed giggles or the bonbons that were tossed out to us in the square in front of the church after a baptism made up for the dreary sermons.

Every day people would scuttle furtively into our house. They would sit around the table while one of the men would go up to the attic and bring down an enormous wireless, as it was then called. Radio-Londres was the real mass that I attended every day. I understood it no better than I did the one celebrated in church, but I listened religiously. To this day I cannot hear the famous theme without getting a lump in my throat, and I hold it against Beethoven that he helped himself to it from the Resistance.

Later the air turned full of the Allied landing. It was imminent, and people spoke of it openly. It was difficult for me to understand the hope vested in this word, *dé-*

barquement. I had never known anything but the German occupation.

I remember how quickly we all closed the shutters that opened onto the street when the enemy troops began their withdrawal. When my mother noticed me in the garden with my nose pressed against the fence, watching the green soldiers pass by, she snatched me out of their sight. They had to abandon their equipment on our side of the river because the bridge had been blown up. Infuriated, they finished off the unfortunate ferryman, who was already in a bad way from the previous war, and waded across on a little dam. The next night we heard shooting in the forest. No one could sleep, whether for fear or for joy.

In the morning, we found swastikas painted on the portals of the church and on the pavement in front of the shop of the butcher woman I liked so much. The priest had the doors scoured, but the tar wouldn't come off, and the spider's shadow remained on the door of God's little house for a long time. The butcher woman was content to throw gravel on her pavement. Lorraine crosses, the symbol of the Resistance fighters, flourished overnight on embroidered armbands that were suspiciously clean, worn by men who strode up the middle of the street and entered the town hall as though they owned it.

The Americans arrived the next day and laid bridges so that their tanks could cross. I cheered them like everyone else. There was no school; what a holiday! I can still see my grandmother Berthe, who had caught up with us, dripping with perspiration, greedily kissing a young GI trapped in his jeep by the crowd. He wiped his face in disgust.

Women with shaved heads were paraded in the streets, some of them with babies in their arms, a few wearing nothing but a slip or a bra and panties. Women guilty of having harbored enemy sperm, whether to feed their children or to celebrate an arrest, whether for a meal or for love, for a pass or a less lonely night, these women of sadness were now offered up to the condemnation of the crowd, which had remained silent for five years. The onlookers gesticulated and screamed at them. Some spat on these third-rate traitors, who are today's grandmas and whose sin was useful in focusing hate and easing unsettled consciences. I, too, raised my little fist.

Actually, I had a happy war. I had my mother all to myself, a woman all to myself. My wish had been granted: I was rid of my rival; I slept in his place in my mother's bed. She found my warm little body reassuring, and I had what every little boy wants most. Every night at the same time I was awakened by the same nightmare, forgotten today. I would bury myself in the warmth and smell of my mother. She treated me a little like the husband she missed, and without realizing it, I was filled with content. I didn't know how dearly I would pay for this first love.

CHAPTER 2

Mama's Boy

It was the postwar that was rough for me.

In Paris, my mother had to put up a long struggle to get our apartment back. The policeman who was living in it was shocked by the idea of having to return it to us. Maybe he liked the place, modest though it was. And maybe he hadn't thought we would ever be back. It was only under duress and with much bitterness that he moved out.

As if to make up for the policeman's attitude, in this twilit France, a good neighbor named Collenot, a dyed-in-the-wool anti-German from the last war, returned those pieces of our furniture which he had salvaged under the Germans' noses and kept in his own small apartment all during the war. The rest had been carried off by helpful Frenchmen, who had gone to a lot of trouble for very little. That same Collenot, whose old army belt and beer belly impressed me, had lent me his grandson's identity at the outset of the Occupation as casually as a soldier lets his buddy use his canteen.

As I was a rickety kid, my mother sent me to a sanatorium by the ocean near Arcachon. The directress would intercept our packages and sell the canned sardines and cookies on the black market; but the assistant directress was kind and generous with the little she had. I was seven years old and just discovering fresh bananas and the pain of separation. The separation was from my mother, to whom I had become addicted during the war. O! those cold dormitory beds! The tearman came by every evening to close our eyes. As for the fresh bananas, I devoured the first one peel and all. My appetite had returned. My mother thought it was due to the good, piney air. Actually, it was because I was free of her.

One day she came to see me with an "uncle." He was a kind man, but I was ferociously jealous. I remember so well that first meeting with my rival and the game of tag we three played on the beach. We were having such a good time until he dared to lay a hand on my mother. In the end, he tamed me.

I returned to liberated Paris, where daily life was more difficult than it had been in the occupied countryside. Keeping warm and fed—everything was a problem; you couldn't find mushrooms or firewood on the city pavements. Above all, I went back to the name Goldberg, which I had never really used before; and I discovered that I was a Jew.

"Dirty Jew! Go back where you came from!" I was stung by the insult every time I heard it—I, who had never been outside of France. That was one of the first lessons I learned in France's lay, free, and compulsory schools. Recess became a nightmare to me. I tried to compensate by being a model pupil, but good grades were no substitute for a little human warmth.

My schoolmates, who had been subjected to intense anti-Semitic propaganda all during the war, did not understand why collaborationist Radio-Paris was now silent. Surrounded by adults who were hardly eager to explain, they continued on the momentum for a good while. Even the teacher took refuge, hiding in an inaccessible room with windows that were opaque up to a man's shoulders. The serpent was dead, but its venom was still active.

"Why is it always me they're after?" I asked my mother. "How am I different from them? How does it show? What is a Jew? Why don't they like Jews? Why, why, why?" My mother didn't know how to answer, or maybe she did and I just didn't understand.

I began to wonder what I had in common with the men who stopped by our place every now and then and hugged me as though they knew me. They would speak to my "uncle" in a language that sounded German, which neither my mother nor I understood. No matter what hour they came, my mother would prepare enormous sandwiches for them; and they would ask for more schnapps, which she ended up serving in jelly glasses. Their conversations were all sprinkled with the same names: Auschwitz, Ravensbrück, Treblinka, Dachau, Buchenwald. They became familiar to me, but I never used them. I began to doubt the meaning of certain words. I thought I knew what a camp was, and I was familiar with terms like "campfire" and "decamp," just as I had been *déporté* by the stream of my beloved river; but suddenly the meanings capsized and these words became heavy with a disturbing mystery. Drancy was hardly less frightening. It was easier to pronounce, but it was not just another Paris suburb. One didn't go there as to Saint-Mandé, and it seemed that, once one was there, it was more difficult to return.

I began to fear these men, who neither laughed nor played with me and for whom the height of tenderness was pinching my cheek until it hurt. They smelled of calamity.

There also surfaced a few old Polish "aunties" who gave wet kisses, whined all the time, and put up with children provided they tiptoed around and asked for second and third helpings of their indigestible *kugelhopf*. It is from them that I learned the expression *françouze tuchess*, French ass, which they used for people they considered alien or hostile: the policeman, who was always suspected of round-ups; the minor civil servant, who lorded it over everyone at his window and claimed that still another paper was missing; the farmer, who made you beg to buy a little butter on the black market and who couldn't tell pure wool from a rayon blend. *Françouze tuchess*—the insult hurt me as much as *kike*.

I could understand why the little pack at Charles Baudelaire School didn't like these people. They were old and they had terrible accents. But me? Why did they find it amusing to block my way out of the washroom and take turns jostling me? I wanted to be part of a group my own age, but they pushed me away from them toward these people who were foreign to me. In my own way, like my grandmother, I too became anti-Semitic.

Many years later, on the high plateau of the Andes, I met a little Aymara Indian playing with a bow and arrow he had made.

"What are you shooting at?" I asked him, laughing.

"Indians, of course!"

His answer struck me as surely as one of his arrows. There is no greater hatred than self-hatred. It prevents one from loving others. It causes suffering that drives one to constant activity. One of the basic motivators of ambition, self-hatred impels one to conquer by admiration what can really be conquered only by affection—"I'm going to show them what I'm worth!" But it is so inefficient a generator: it runs continuously, but with such poor yields, and, above all, it leads one ever farther—higher, some say—always more alone. Already, I had nothing but my dear books.

I spent six uneventful years at the lycée, accumulating merit badges. It hardly entered our minds then to protest the gray walls, the stupid monitors, the droning declensions. And when we peed on Philip Augustus's venerable wall, we were challenging neither History nor France.

Three of the pimpled kids of these years scraped their way through the lycée with me. Surprisingly enough, I didn't shed even one of them en route, undoubtedly because they were inseparable. They always sat together, giggled together, were rescued together, copying one another's stupidities. Their names were Ramin, Mazot, and Bonasse, which quickly became condensed to Ramass. Together they sniggered loudly whenever our history or physics instructor uttered the word *period*; they guffawed whenever a teacher addressed the boy unfortunate enough to be named Peter; and they fell over laughing every time a teacher tried to make a joke.

It was Ramass—I don't know which one of the trio—who asked me, as I was about to leave for the only skiing trip I took during my adolescence: "Why is it always the Jews who can afford winter sports?" It was Ramass again who, one day when we were walking along together, stopped under a music-hall poster which proudly announced: "Rita dances in the nude."

"She's a Jew," he said. "My father told me. . . . He knows, he works for the subway system . . . not punching tickets, in the office." How could I contradict such irrefutable proof of my race's moral turpitude?

On the whole, the anti-Semitism that I encountered at the lycée was less direct than in primary school. There were fewer insults and more innuendoes, the true basis of which I did not always understand. I still wondered what my classmates had against me, how I differed from them.

All the more so since I was different from other Jews. There were some others at the lycée, but they were of little help to me in defining or defending myself. At least they had the Torah to treasure and Atonement to cleanse their souls once a year; they knew why they were insulted and where to take refuge.

18

Faced with so much injustice, I tried everything. I tried to argue my way to friendship. I tried to buy it by passing my Latin translation to an idiot who copied it so slavishly that we were both caught. I tried to inspire fear by inventing a brown belt in judo for myself. Nothing worked. It was on my seat that they stuck chewing gum; it was my shoelaces that they knotted together in the cloakroom; I was the one they asked how it felt to have some of it cut off.

One afternoon, while I was waiting for a bus, a group of older boys came noisily running down the street, whirling their school bags over their heads like maces. Just as the bus arrived, one of them snatched my queue ticket from my hand and rushed toward the bus. A rather shabbily dressed old man with a shopping bag in his hand came over to me and asked, in a strong accent, "Are you a yid?" It was clear that he wanted to help me, but only if I was one of his tribe. "No," I replied instinctively.

Today, I still wonder about this denial. Did I feel alien toward the old man? Did I fear retaliation? Was I against adults interfering in children's internal affairs? Perhaps all of these. At any rate, I lost my place, and the old man, a little surprised, went on his way.

For a long time I found it comfortable to blame my classmates' hostility on anti-Semitism alone. But now I believe that the main reason they didn't like me was that I was a mama's boy. So it was only a question of striking where it was easiest, where they knew it would hurt the most.

My mother wanted to remarry, but she had no real proof of my father's death. The law was not adapted to the technology of the Final Solution, to those deaths without dates, without corpses, without burials, and without witnesses. A report of my family council dated 1948 refers to the death of "Goldberg, Joseph, on the twenty-eighth of December nineteen hundred and forty-four at Auschwitz, *where he happened to be momentarily.*" One is tempted to add, "vacationing," as though his death were unrelated to the place. One must admire the precision of the date; only the hour is missing. In fact, my mother had found two Auschwitz survivors who were willing to give false testimony. And so she was able to marry my "uncle."

For a while she lived in a mélange of hope and anxiety. Some former deportees, "liberated" by the Soviets, had reappeared years after the end of the war. But the statistics were against my father, and gradually he sank into the six million without changing the total, without ceremony. Since I had never mourned him, he had never left me; mourning, burial—these are not for the dead but for the living. There was never a place I could go to commune with his spirit, so I carried his grave with me everywhere, always.

How I would have liked to push the creaking gate of an old cemetery and walk among the marble and pots of flowers to the grave where my father's bones would be resting, pull up an impious weed and then leave, each one of us, the dead and the living, at peace in his own world. Even that had been denied me, and I felt a stranger among those vaults where generations formed a human chain, before the list of the dead engraved in the heart of each village, reciting the official litany of those who had lived there. Having no village of their own, Jews were condemned to wander even in death. I didn't know on what date to mourn my father so I mourned him any old time, whenever I felt sad or too happy, whenever I missed him or felt guilty for not missing him.

My father became the offspring of my imagination. I created and re-created him at will, each time stronger, more intelligent, more absent than before. At the age when children hide behind their fathers, I invented one who could fence effortlessly with all the fathers invoked by my adversaries. Only he never came to get me when school let out. I always crossed alone that no-man's-land between school and home, where children settle their scores.

My mother, with all her rage, wanted to pretend that the war had never existed. She wanted her second husband to adopt me. She had another son, and she wanted both of us to bear the same name, a non-Jewish name to protect us from a new pogrom. In spite of legal obstacles, she achieved her goal and assumed the divine right to name.

To spare me from perhaps being massacred later, she undertook to destroy me on the spot. I was stripped of my private though very common surname. It was like killing the father a second time. His name was pierced from end to end by a straight red line drawn in the family record. And I consented—I was an accomplice—to this murder of a dead man. It was also something of a suicide, even then.

I found myself masquerading under a name that didn't really exist, a name without precedent, without roots, without an echo, a stump of a name with a final *t* grafted onto it to make it more French. It was Cojot, the name of my mother's new husband, the man who had taken my father's place and mine. Cojot, Michel Cojot, was born.

But my real name, Goldberg, was my last visible link with Jewishness, my last external sign of belonging, the sign by which I was recognized, even if only to be reviled. At least I existed. In agreeing to cast my true identity into limbo, I sided with those who had insulted me. From now on they would treat me as though I were their accomplice. I became one of them. Each of their manifestations of contempt toward Jews found me paralyzed by that forged name. The new name, acceptable everywhere because it came from nowhere, gave me access to the anti-Semitic world.

My Jewishness receded to a small piece of flesh that is generally hidden from view, stamp and seal of the Covenant. Still, I always felt the need to identify myself to the women I knew. No doubt I was afraid that I might find myself in the arms of one or the other who would love me while detesting Jews. It was also a way of making them change their minds.

My definition of a Jew went beyond those of Sartre— "anyone who is known as a Jew"—and the rabbis— "anyone whose mother was a Jew." My definition was circumstantial, malodorous: "Whoever has gone or would have gone to the oven is a Jew." Baptized Jews like Max Jacob, anti-Semitic Jews like Simone Weil, atheistic Jews like my father, hidden Jews, ashamed Jews, ostentatious Jews, little Jews, big Jews, average Jews, all were united and joined together in the smoke of Birkenau, which knew only one distinction: white smoke for those who had been there for some time, dark for the newcomers, who still had a little fat on their bones.

I borrowed the definition from the Nazis, who were not much mistaken on this count. But it was empty, empty of culture, empty of history except that of the Pogrom of pogroms—empty of faith, empty of love. Mine was only a fraternity of suffering. My community was only of the dead.

As son of a French war casualty, I was "Adopted by the Nation," but I was rejected by the majority of Frenchmen; a Jew rejecting Jews, the lonely child became a lonely man. This was a source of pain and pride. I no longer had a place in any tribe. I no longer had a tribe.

I knew only one intermission in this solitude: during my first stay in the United States, my first act of independence from my mother. I had received a scholarship to a high school in the Far West. I discovered a desert which was painted, sunsets that took my breath away, saguaro cactus with flowers that had taken eight years to bloom reaching toward the heavens; Navajo, Pima, Hopi, and even a few Apache who had climbed down from the movie screen for a chocolate shake at the corner drugstore; the sunwashed winter, the inaccessible Canyon de Chelly, and that other canyon, so deep that the colors of its walls tell the story of the Earth all the way back to infancy.

But it was neither the beauty of America nor its surprises that caused my attachment to that country. For the first time in my life I felt fully French. I had to travel over four thousand miles to be accepted as French, without having my nationality attenuated because I was Jewish.

Only America was capable of such a reception. This is why, in spite of the flatness of Kansas and the squareness of Main Street, the movie houses smelling of popcorn, the pink plastic curlers, Mona Lisa eating cheeseburgers, social insecurity, the Daughters of the American Revolution, toilets without doors and neon churches, economic smugness and monetary incontinence, I am infinitely grateful to her.

But still, I missed France. On my return, I resumed my place in the ranks of the outcasts, of those who are repeatedly asked for dues which are never enough. Back home again, I was a stranger. I could no longer be myself. I could no longer be.

CHAPTER 3 *The "Ogg"*

Since I couldn't be, I had to do. I was very successful at it. From first-class honors on graduating from the lycée to valedictorian of a near-Grande Ecole, from attending a renowned American university before it was the thing to do to joining the inner circle of banking, from missions to the four corners of the world to lunch with undersecretaries.

But every time I reached a goal, it lost all value for me. Had I passed my examinations? I was lucky, and besides, they weren't that difficult. Had I received a flattering promotion? It suited my boss, and anyway, the title was more important than the substance of the job. In short, I never admitted to having any merit, though of course that did not prevent me from being considered arrogant.

From success to success, I felt only defeat. I always needed to achieve more. I never lived in the present. I steered a course between the night and fog* of the past and the revenge of the future. I dreamed only of power, knowl-

---

Nuit et Brouillard was a famous Resnais film whose title was taken from the Nazis' code name for their extermination operations.

edge, and combat. My mother had taught me the lesson she had learned: how to fight when you are weak. So I fought everything, everyone, including myself. I saw the world only in terms of power relationships. Knowing that I was weak, I built a thick wall behind which I lived protected. Blows could not reach me, but neither could feelings. They could not enter or leave. I was like one of those animals without a backbone which are actually held together only by their shells.

I did not realize then that the quest for power, prestige, money, and glory is nothing more than an indirect attempt to conquer love, an attempt used by the handicapped who cannot obtain it naturally. An exhausting quest, doomed to failure. It is never enough. I was incapable of loving and didn't know it. Anyway, what I then perceived as love seemed to me weakness. I saw its effects on my fellow students who, from one day to the next, neglected their studies, which I believed to be of much greater importance. That wouldn't happen to me.

Love in my eyes was a sham, an invention of idle Western women, hypocrisy masking physical need. I even went so far as to write, for my own amusement, a play about an engineer who could have been my twin brother. Tired of hearing his wife ask him if he loves her, he invents the "aphrometer," a love-measuring instrument, so that he can answer her question with precision.

Still, I had relations with women; but I wanted to be loved without having to love in return. The women were always older, almost always blond, and, with one half-exception, never Jewish. I was shrewd enough to justify any one of these characteristics. Not one of my rationalizations was valid, but it didn't matter. One of the women, who was either more candid or more clear-sighted than the others, lovingly called me a grocer. As a matter of fact, I did weigh my caresses and measure my words of affection, cheated on quality and gave no change.

Sexuality would not be worth dwelling on if it were just another bodily function. But it is the mirror of the soul, the exposed part of the personality, the only one that meshes so directly with the unconscious. Self-perpetuation is the basic goal of life; and here, between our legs, is the instrument of our deepest drives in charge of our private justice, rewards and punishments.

I did not make love, I demonstrated power. And also indifference. I remember a woman fifteen years my senior whose letters, which I still have, are proof that she loved me. She yearned for long embraces, and I made a habit of putting a book on the pillow near her head while she tried to find pleasure. I lent her my body but kept my mind for more important things; my time was too precious to waste in romps. It was thus that I read a good portion of Robert Aron's *Histoire de Vichy*. If that woman reads this book, I ask her pardon, and Aron's as well.

One summer evening, while I was sitting on a bench in the little Place de Furstenberg, I noticed a pretty blonde being annoyed by a pest. Why was she rejecting him? Why did she seem to be asking me for help? Why did this unknown girl seem so grateful when I walked straight toward her as though we had a date, causing her would-be suitor to take off in embarrassment? Why me and not him? That is how I met Marie-France, with the soft eyes, sometimes gray, sometimes green. We had so little in common, but we were the exact complements of each other.

Marie-France had attended the proper schools, but her ignorance of the world was immense. She lived in a bubble full of dreams, music, and novels. Newspapers, licenses, applications, the daily struggle for life were completely foreign to her. The product of parents who had succeeded in piling on her the disadvantages of both petit-bourgeois and working-class education, she had learned neither needlepoint nor dressmaking, neither pastry decoration nor cooking, neither law nor bookkeeping, neither bridge nor Old Maid, neither sailing nor rollerskating. Unattended to, ignored in favor of a sickly elder brother who was the focus of all motherly concern, she had concluded that one had to be ill in order to be pampered.

Her father, who flaunted the "de" in his name like a boutonnière, had little time for her. He was a framer of works of art—emphasis on "art." Behind his Windsor tie lived both a small businessman and an artist, a leading citizen and a dauber. He summoned me to his office for a sort of entrance examination. There was no doubt about the outcome, of course, but for an unusual half-hour he insisted on playing the role of the heavy father. To seem in order to be.

Pot-bellied and with hair disheveled, he was onstage: "You know, we are very broad-minded. In spite of the differences in background, we believe that only the individual matters, and you have much to recommend you. Moreover, since my daughter loves you. . . . You understand, of course, the need for a marriage contract, even if *today* there is no property to be divided? Besides, there are not only financial clauses. We could include something about baptism of the children, for example."

Seated on the edge of the chair that my father should have occupied, I silently took the brunt of the words that were uttered as well as those that were not.

The schools that my wife-to-be had attended were devoted primarily to enhancing the status of the parents and secondarily to delaying their children's introduction to four-letter words. They also allowed a few mustachioed spinsters, who confused hatred of men with love of God, to satisfy their sadistic tendencies by picking on helpless children. Transforming a religion of love into an instrument of torture, instead of B.A.s or saints they turned out anticlerics. They did an admirable job of nurturing my innocent fiancée's penchant for guilt. Every week she had to invent sins for confession on Friday. By the time I met her, she was perfectly prepared to atone for those she had not committed.

Nevertheless, despite her lack of a degree and of a profession, this unlearned woman knew something that I did not: she knew how to love. Love was as natural to her as breathing, and she thought it was just as natural to others, therefore to me. If I didn't know how to breathe, all she had to do was show me how. Each of us hoped to change the other. She didn't know too much? So much the better; she would owe everything to me. I would mold her to my twisted measure.

And it was I, small-time Pygmalion, who taught her to drive, to swim, to write a check, to take a photograph, to eat with chopsticks. I took her to the ends of the earth, though she didn't ask for it, but failed to give her what mattered most. I sent her to that school which had apparently agreed with me: the school of humiliation. Without knowing it, I took revenge on this sweet, clear-eyed Gentile. Not so much for the German enemies whom I had hardly known and with whom she had very little in common, but rather for the average Frenchman, who had not wanted me as a brother.

My wife was so French, so difficult to export, with her snub nose, her taste for champagne and whirling waltzes, her family home that was impossible to heat, her respect for titles, her lack of respect for the authorities, her auntie-who-didn't-like-Jews, her great-grandfather who was a blacksmith, her homemaking grandmothers and her wise patriarch, loyal to General de Gaulle after having sworn allegiance to Marshal Pétain.

I gave Marie-France a permanent demonstration of the superiority of the *üntermensch*. Without realizing it, I undertook to destroy her—and myself in the process, for her humiliation was also mine. I had chosen as a wife a woman so vulnerable that I had the unconscious certainty that even during the worst of quarrels she would not hurl the damned insult; it was as though I had married a German or a black or a Jewess. She was my racial security. Had she resisted me she might have saved us both; but she was so eager to be castigated. She had never believed in her absolution.

Why did Marie-France hate herself to the point of choosing a scourge-husband? Why her need, wherever there was light, to hide her rather pretty face under the blues, reds, or creams that I called her paints? Why her fear of the morning, of the sun, of rainwater, seawater, or table water, of the wind that tousled her hair? Why her attraction to dark rooms, evenings that run into the morning, and men with troubled souls? She was so badly in need of a man to replace her father, who was absent even when he was there, a male who could calm the hollow feeling in the stomach that we call anguish, a warrior who would protect her and punish her for having wished harm to her abusive brother.

No couple stays together unless each partner gets his or her due out of the relationship. Unions between neurotics are, if not the most beautiful, among the most solid. I wanted to chastise, my wife wanted to be chastised. A horrible game in which both are instruments of torture, the punishment of the other and of self, in which each one suffers through and for the other.

Having thus begun my career as a husband-scourge, welcomed with half-opened arms into my wife's family, my new family, I had to earn a living, I had to conquer, I had to do.

I took my banking vows as I had my marriage ones, driven by the unconscious desire to be accepted by the world that had rejected me when I was Goldberg. Marie-France de . . . and the Banque des . . . were bits of France—of old France, so old that it seemed bound to last forever. I made the same career mistake that Dreyfus had. I too became a captain.

Five or six years of study in institutions where the learning was not so high spared me fifteen years behind a window, filling out forms, scrounging for money by the middle of the month, and transferring from one provincial town to another. I started at headquarters in Paris, five stories above the window tellers who so impress the people who really need money.

In charge of Planning and Methods, I had the job of searching the ever-receding horizon—1970, 1980, 1985, 1990. I painted it in dark colors, populated it with pincer rates, clamoring employees, squeezed margins, fickle or bankrupt clients, foreign bankers wading ashore holding their attaché cases above their heads.

I described a bank suffocating under a mountain of checks, tied down by sadistic-liberal regulations, invaded by an army of long-haired employees and computer experts speaking Cobol, Fortran, and even English. Such would be the results since a cabinet minister who imagined he was Saint-Just and still revered Adam Smith had succeeded in introducing vile competition into one of the few structures of Vichy to survive the Liberation.

But no one really believed it, not even I. Everyone secretly felt that the bank, like France, was eternal and that he had a little piece of that eternity. Competition— that was easy to say, banking would never become the Flea Market. Banking wasn't open to just anyone. And then there was the State. Prosperous banks were useful to the State: low-cost loans for its sagging enterprises; savings, not too well compensated, that would be dissipated by the tax on prudence called inflation, helped along, if necessary, by investment counselors; jobs for those unemployed who agreed to cut their hair until the end of their probationary period and, especially, for a few high-level civil servants who would consent to the trebling of their salaries to instill the illusion of public interest in institutions populated by others who so regret not having been born into government service.

It didn't take me long to persuade myself that the work I was doing was useless. My horizon was five years, the loan officers' was ninety days, and the bank president's, the next government shake-up, unless he emulated Gauguin, who had the guts to abandon the stock market for the South Seas. The only sympathetic response came from colleagues who, like me, were constantly making another study and who were isolated from the heart of banking. And, nevertheless, we were paid and even given raises after painstaking and ritualistic ceremonies. To avoid displeasing inflation fighters or swelling the pyramid with local favors, we varied the number of months in the year rather than the amount of the monthly salary. Thus the pay slips had twenty-seven columns for years with sixteen and a half months. In addition, there were bonuses—a balance-sheet bonus, a basement bonus, distance allowances, layette allowances, shoe allowances, risk premiums, an end-of-year bonus, a mid-year bonus (called the vacation bonus); there were even "one-time" bonuses, which came year after year. Of course, in this way, the employees became the bank's creditors, but if they requested advances on their bonuses the computers would hum with pleasure.

In short, the bank enjoyed a peaceful existence, dozing on its reserves, its legal reserves, its supplementary reserves, its hidden reserves, reserves for risks, and reserves for nothing at all. The only thing that could bring a momentary thrill was a hold-up.

I bridled with impatience at so much inertia. It was humiliating to profit from and be an example of all this waste. I eased my conscience by working with a zeal that may have endeared me to my superiors but provoked annoyance from my colleagues and poorly disguised irritation from my subordinates. First in my class again, I was again alone with my clear conscience. I applied the methods that had worked so well for me at school to my work at the bank, but the rules of the game were different. It was no longer a question of succeeding alone against all the others but *with* others.

Unable to make my sense of order prevail at the bank, I tried to establish it at home. I was the master of details, the weekend sergeant, the controller of overspending and of the refrigerator. I tried to manage my home as I wanted to see the bank managed, with a budget, forecasts, records—in short, anti-Marie-France.

One evening during a bitter quarrel, my wife yelled at me: "It's a pity you're Jewish, you would have made a good Nazi!" She had previously used a variant in which I "would have made a good Christian." For her, that was almost as strong. I had suffered, I had to make others suffer in return. Of all the people toward whom I might have directed my hostility, my wife deserved it least. But isn't it true that torturers choose victims who are weak and innocent? Do they even choose?

God, how suspect are mixed marriages! When a distinguished black man marries a white sales clerk, is it a sign of lack of prejudice or, on the contrary, the addition of social to racial prejudice? Does his prestige make it easier for her to accept his color? Does her fair skin make it easier for him to accept her modest status?

This terrible equation did not cross my mind at the time. My only thoughts were of shaping this raw material. I did not see that in marrying a non-Jew I had continued the task of self-destruction, calling a halt to twenty centuries of suffering but also of courage; putting an end to my history, I gave mute testimony that those who had done me harm were right. "Spouses of Aryans" had generally escaped deportation since they themselves had programmed their own dilution, their own disappearance. My marriage was my contribution to the Final Solution. Through my children, I would pass the invisible but very real line of demarcation once and for all, even if I refused to have them baptized as my clerical-socialist father-in-law wished.

Like her name, her eyes, like France herself, there were two sides to Marie-France, morning and evening, laughter and anguish, that which loved me and that which detested me, that which I loved and that which I detested. She passed from one to the other without warning or awareness. Every evening when I put the key in the lock I felt a twinge of uneasiness: which one would I find? She knew so well how to punish me for leaving her alone.

There was a great deal of love between us, but I was incapable of expressing mine except by causing her to suffer. That makes me a sadist.

One day after a long horseback ride I had to dash to the train without even changing clothes. Reflected in the windows of the station at Poitiers was an image which, though a little fuzzy, brought back a memory. I could see the flat stomach and short hair, the feet firmly planted, the riding crop teasing shiny black boots. I closed my eyes, trying to keep my balance. I looked like an SS.

How easy it is to find the road back to the camp that I have never known. The barracks, the striped uniforms, the stacked-up bunks, the latrines, the watchtowers, "Los! los! los!," the dogs, the rain, the wind, the mud, the Work Makes One Free sign on the gate, the roll calls, the screams, the hanged ones forbidden to stick out their tongues, the lowered eyes, even the smell, the smell of flesh burning after the horrified soul has escaped. And the masters of the place and the time, of life and death. I resembled them, on the outside as well as on the inside. Tired of being oppressed, I had unwittingly chosen the torturer's camp. I had come to resemble my enemy.

Marie-France talked to me about love until she was out of kisses, but I couldn't accept anything she said because she was who she was. Imagine a deportee trying to convince an SS that he was on the wrong path.

As I traveled the world, her letters followed me. "My love, my darling," she wrote, "take good care of yourself today, don't forget that you are my life. . . ." "Be good, my darling, I am so happy to be your wife. . . ." "Don't worry about me, the love I have for you makes me feel rich." "Without you, I feel more and more like a plant that someone has forgotten to water. . . ." "Haven't you realized yet how nice tenderness is?"

I would stuff these letters into my pocket, not without having made a mental note of the spelling mistakes. I did not, could not, understand. Let this idle woman love me; I had better things to do.

I frightened her. She nicknamed me the "ogg," her childish pronunciation of "ogre."

CHAPTER 4 *Blind Alley*

The bank's managing directorship was open, and in plain sight of everyone the two assistant managing directors indulged in one of those cockfights that send tremors through the headquarters of a company. Each of the two candidates had his own rather well-defined area, in which there was no lack of work. Nevertheless, each launched periodic forays into the other's territory, causing him to raise his hackles for retaliation. For a long time I had been convinced that conflict was the rule in the upper echelons of corporations, with every male thus responding to a vital need to prove his superiority. But how tedious are these shoot-outs in which no one dies!

Each man—the aristocrat, confident of his good taste, and the self-made man, scarred from his rise—had his special talents and qualities, but both demanded loyalty even more than competence from their subordinates. It was necessary to choose sides and make one's allegiance known. Since I had to work with both, I tried to remain on good terms with each, with the result that neither trusted me. Whoever became managing director, I could expect nothing from him.

As a matter of fact, I began to wish that things would become difficult for the bank, that all of us would stop wasting energy in internal disputes, that all hands would go on deck, fight it out, and let the better men win. I could not believe that my life was largely played out and that all I had left to do was drift toward retirement—the social death that the Spaniards call "jubilation." What a prospect!

In the various committee meetings that I was expected to attend—the Management Committee, the Monday Committee, the Investment Committee—I met veterans for whom a seat at the heavy conference table was a lifelong dream come true. What was said in the meetings mattered little to these men; for them the main thing was to be there. Having left school too early, they were condemned for life to listen to well-polished presentations by former top students. It was worse than being forced to stand in the corner but much better paid.

Actually, these men *were* the bank. They knew who made money and how, the money that was needed to pay such high salaries to the president and the other wits who had never approached a prospect; to install air-conditioned headquarters in the best section of Paris, with a cafeteria-aquarium and a tapestried, wood-paneled, carpeted, chandeliered, busted, and Louis XV-clocked conference room; to provide tenured employment for all, even the lazy, the incompetent, the insubordinate, or the pincher of secretarial bottoms; to finance tribal wars between branches and headquarters, marketers and back-office workers, bottom-line bankers at the top and foot soldiers at the bottom, cocky Parisians and provincial clods, Montagues and Capulets.

The president, a high-ranking civil servant in exile for whom government business was the only business, always tried to raise the level of discussion, which was a way of emphasizing the distance between himself and the coarse, self-taught men and of sparing himself the need to make decisions in areas in which he was wise enough to know that he was ignorant. The professional bankers were concerned with making and collecting loans; he was concerned with the impact of decisions on the money supply and on his comrades in the Ministry of Finance.

The Investment Committee meeting dragged on and on. It would be almost another hour before everyone, hungry or not, went off to lunch, at the bank's and taxpayers' expense, in the restaurant that corresponded to his place in the hierarchy, to take two hours to settle what could have been solved in ten minutes, or simply to chatter pompously with an associate, a colleague—bankers do not have competitors—or some other gray- or blue-suited executive he knew from college, "the club," or a summer in Provence.

The Michel Cojot I was at work sometimes found it difficult to prevent his mind from sneaking out the door imprudently left ajar by the usher who delivered messages or brought in mineral water. When his thoughts returned, he would glance through his diary as a silent way of suggesting that things be speeded up. That would keep his hands still for a moment and interrupt his pencil's impertinent rambling over his note pad. To appear more serious, he would jot down a few figures—calculating the cost of the meeting per minute, for example. He had to act out his role, even if the play didn't have any great plot but just many small ones, full of repetition and, above all, tedious. I would never last another quarter of a century.

It was going to be my turn to speak. As I went over the three points of my statement in my mind, I could already hear myself speaking in a firm voice and with the right adjectives. I liked these exercises, even if I knew how futile they were; we wouldn't use this or any other method to decide whether it would be better to open a new branch in Carpentras or Romorantin or one more around the Champs Elysées or, *res horrenda auditu*, to close one. If the Nationale des Dépôts, the Française de Crédits, or the Industrielle de Banque did it, we had to do it too, that was that, or risk losing market share. And if no one else did it, what good would it be to do it alone? A study of the desirability of opening a branch would take six months and alert the competition, which would grab the best locations and drive up the price of others. . . . At any rate, bank profits in those happy days were such that any branch, once opened, quickly became profitable. Everyone was convinced that this proliferation of piggy banks was a waste, but since others were doing it, one had to follow suit and sometimes lead.

Seated around the table, dark-suited, clean-shaven, we listened to our president a little the way officials of the Fourth Republic listened to their new minister. We knew that he would pass and we would remain. Suddenly, I was observing myself from the outside, both attentive and indifferent to the tirade. Michel Cojot, banker. Michel Cojot, with eight layers of fabric around his neck. What would happen if he were to disappear? There would hardly be a ripple on the surface of the bank. Michel Cojot, seated next to Vérard, a former member of the Action Française,* who had had a few problems at the time of the Liberation. Others for whom the big event of 1943 was the transfer to Saint-Étienne or the kid's scarlet fever. And others whom Cojot liked and who also worked like dogs without believing much in what they were doing.

I asked myself why I was there. Images surfaced in me, as violent as sobs. I saw the child I once was, playing marbles, gathering mushrooms in the moist grass, the same child whose mother had such trouble consoling him the day Jack London's White Fang died on the icy steppes of Hudson Bay.

Michel Cojot the banker. Was it really me? Overpaid, overprotected, respected by those on the outside, regarded, feared, or envied by those on the inside, what was my complaint? If I wasn't happy, I had only to resign.

I wanted to be on the firing line. But what is a firing line in time of peace? I wanted to offer my blood, but there

*A prewar right-wing organization discredited by its association with Vichy.

were no takers. This place was too cushy, its air too rarefied; it was too much given to thoughts—of the proper kind—too little to action. I decided to chuck it. I had had enough of being lost in overhead costs, in fixed costs, in unproductive costs. Someone suggested that I try to recover a few petrodollars at the outskirts of the Empire— that I go to Latin America.

Marie-France was a trooper; she followed her man into battle. Besides, she was none the worse for it. I continued to play the role of family sergeant with good conscience. Living only for my work, I considered a good bottle of wine, a good meal, a stroll, a concert, a summer novel, a lazy morning to be signs of greed and weakness, a waste of time. Shame on pleasure-seekers!

Only striving found favor with me. I was a workaholic. Though there was no real need for it, I worked at night, on weekends, on Christmas Day. Enough to make everyone who did not work as much as I feel guilty. I became a regular disturber of the night watchmen's naps and a familiar figure to the battalion of gap-toothed cleaning women. When I was taking my wife to the hospital to have our second baby, I made a detour to leave a document at the bank, at the risk that she would give birth in the car. Work was a drug for me, as it is for so many other hard-pedaling executives; but I made it a virtue.

Moreover, I was faithful to my wife; well, almost.

At the end of a difficult assignment in Africa, I had given up all hope of obtaining certain documents that I had been promised on at least ten occasions. I was packing my bags in my room, separated from the sea by two rows of palm trees swaying in the dust-filled desert wind, when there was a knock on the door. It was a beautiful black woman dressed in a traditional robe; I had caught a glimpse of her earlier in some important person's waiting room.

"Here are your papers," she said.

"Thank you, it is kind of you to bring them. Who sent you?"

"No one."

"What do you mean, no one?"

"I heard you ask for them several times. I didn't think it was right to give you the runaround like that . . . I knew where they were . . . You see, we are not all alike."

She had brought me a gift, a little *balafon*. My first thought was not very charitable. "Careful," I said to myself. "She has probably been sent by someone to try to compromise you." My second hypothesis was more plausible, I believe, even if it may have been too flattering to my ego. She was probably motivated by the desire to please, to show the white man that, unlike her masters of the moment, she did not approve of petty acts of revenge. She wanted the white man's respect, she wanted the white man's love, she was my Jew.

What all my arguments and veiled threats had failed to obtain was offered to me by this woman who had nothing to gain. I took a bottle of perfume out of my bag, purchased on the plane for Marie-France, and handed it to her. I gave her a long kiss, fondled her breasts, which, to my surprise, were enclosed in an ordinary bra, and escorted her to the door.

Why hadn't I taken this woman, who had made herself available in this way? There was no lack of good arguments; Work and Family were not bad ones. But deep inside me, I realized that my wife had won a monopoly over my virility. I discovered that I was fitted with a chastity belt to which, without knowing it, she held the key.

I did not accept this sanction. Was I sentenced to one woman forever? And why Marie-France, with whom my relations were so difficult, so unequal? What if I wanted to leave her, to divorce her, or simply to punish her—punish her for holding me back in my rise up the ladder, punish her for always being sick when it was least convenient for me, punish her for loving me, for her new monopoly?

We left Paris for Ciudad Nueva, and for a while I immersed myself in the change. After a few reservations, of course, Marie-France proved to be receptive to my arguments when I suggested that we move: "First of all," she wrote me, "I think I have stored up enough courage to cope with exile again. Besides, I have decided that it is probably better for me to be as you want me to be, and make you almost happy, than to be some kind of lazy courtesan who likes living from night to day and dancing and laughing more than anything and who is ill suited to the man-with-problems that you are.

"White flag, surrender, the slave revolt is over. I hope, sir, that you will find me an obedient little girl with no will other than yours. No doubt there will be times when my confounded nostalgia for the young woman who talks like a snob, reads only novels, gives in to her vices, and believes that she can escape the nitty-gritty will return to the surface; but I am sure that you will help me to subdue this trio of women, the lazy, the scatterbrained, the sensuous."

I was not aware of driving her to destroy herself. Without understanding it, I watched her become her own kapo. I paid much more attention to what was happening to me, and I had not yet forgotten my African nonadventure. I decided to clear it up in my own mind.

One weekend when I was in Mexico—Marie-France had remained behind in Ciudad Nueva—I paid a visit to Oaxaca, the beautiful jade town dear to Malcolm Lowry and his lost Yvonne. The smells of the market, the spicy tacos, the antiquated colonial buildings, the feathered dancers as on the posters—everything rang true. I dragged my solitude to the local pyramids, where at last I began a real conversation—with one of those women who hide their disappointment for not resembling Elizabeth Taylor by making no effort to look attractive. Besides, what an eloquent way to indicate that they want to be loved for the mind. I hesitated, but the desire to betray my wife with a woman much less beautiful than she got the better of me. A few hours later, we walked past the scandalized face of the no doubt virtuous young woman ensconced behind the mahogany reception desk of my hotel.

I, whom no one had ever resisted, I, who was listened to with attention, admiration, or fear—I was incapable of doing what the lowliest of peons do—too often for the liking of demographers. My companion of the moment seemed to attach little importance to the matter, but I believed that her kindness was a pretense.

I felt angry with this servant who no longer obeyed, crushed by the notions, commonplace and mostly false, that flourish in this secret garden of the soul. I began to wish that this foreign woman would go far away, taking the secret of my infirmity with her. Everything around me was alive—the toddlers, the dogs, the flies, the macaws, the hips of the Indian women swaying slowly under their skirts, their breasts pressed down against blouses that would have pleased Matisse, addressing the message of life to one and all. I felt excluded. But why? I was strong, well fed, never ill. What was wrong?

I didn't know then that to have desire, I needed to feel secure—that is, loved. How could I have known it since I didn't believe in love? I believed only in power and in intelligence in the service of power.

Even the way I mounted a horse betrayed me. I had no appreciation of the animal or of nature. I was insensitive to the relaxing pleasure of the walk or of a well-gaited trot. I liked only galloping, first the canter, which welds animal and man together as prelude to the charge, which releases energy long pent up in both man and beast, the pelvis of one guiding the effort of the other. I liked mixing my breath and sweat with those of the animal imprisoned between my thighs. I liked dominating the horse just as I liked dominating a woman. I liked mastering something stronger than I, conquering my fear in the face of an obstacle. I was proud of having stayed in the saddle after my horse reared its head, gashing my chin.

All I had to do to win the admiration of the *charros* of Chihuahua was to mount one of their horses, on which each instant was a struggle. These men, who had inherited Arab values via Andalusia, considered me their equal: one more little macho in this beautiful land of Mexico, where there are already so many.

"Walk or freeze," I said during our honeymoon trip to my young wife, who, exhausted by too long a stroll, had slumped into the deep snow. It was getting dark and cold, and the snow was too soft for me to carry her. She walked.

I admit that she didn't always toe the line. She made a habit of falling ill at times that forced me to choose between her and my obligation of the moment. It happened on at least ten occasions. Once, when I was about to leave on a trip, suspicious lumps appeared on her body requiring immediate surgery. It was not a feigned illness; it was an appeal. I paid for the best specialist and the best hospital for her and ran off to catch my plane.

It was the dialogue between the fish in the water and the fish in the air. The first is incapable of imagining a world without water, without love; the other, who has always heard of water but has never tasted it, is restless. He tosses and turns, endlessly seeking something—he doesn't know what—which he never finds. The fool suffers so much that he imagines the world is concerned with no one but him. He continues to toss, and his life becomes one long obstacle course.

Everything will be better after the exam, after the appointment, after the first million, after the victory, always after, after, after. But once the fleeting intoxication of success has passed, the problems resurface. The hurdle wasn't high enough. Let's raise it again: a second million, a new promotion, another decoration, another victory; after Austria, Czechoslovakia; after Poland, France, Russia, the world, the universe!

I had already cleared so many hurdles without being satisfied. I needed another one, a real one this time, not just any old hedge but a wall, a high wall.

More degrees? Certainly not. I didn't know what to do with those I already had. The main reason for having them, I had decided, was to justify to others, to those who were excluded, the privileges enjoyed by graduates. But degrees are not an end in themselves, and besides, I was past the age.

More money? I had never truly given any thought to the deeper meaning of money. I hadn't noticed yet that Harpagon speaks of the purse purloined from him as he would of a woman who had been stolen from him. Nevertheless, to exchange the numbered days of one's life for ever-higher stacks of paper seemed to me a foolish and contemptible trade. I was surrounded by people with more money than they needed. I didn't admire them for it, often the contrary.

Power? Perhaps, but what sort of power and how? Economic power was of little interest to me. I did not envy my bosses, whom I had so often seen bound hand and foot by "the profession," hobbled by their stockholders, paralyzed by their barons, the unions, their own comrades, or the supreme yoke of the Administration. Exasperated by the large number of ushers in the main entrance hall, which he was powerless to reduce, an important director found that the only way to avoid them was to get to his office through the entrance reserved for minor employees.

Political power? The essence of power. The quest for love in a democracy, conquest by force in a dictatorship; the paranoid's siren song, supreme aphrodisiac, illusory victory over death, stepladder to the immortality of a street-corner plaque. But I had neither tribe nor identity. How could I hope to lead people who did not even recognize me as one of them?

I went round in circles. I was rotting in my traces. Lately, I had had deep and diffuse pain in two fingers of my right hand, the forefinger and the middle finger. I made doctors on two continents richer. The best of them were honest enough to tell me that they could do nothing for me. My problem, in this world of specialists, was knowing which one to go to. The rheumatologist injected, the surgeon cut, others fumbled their way around. They opened up my hand to see what the problem was; they saw what it was not. It was not venereal, or Dupuytren's, or tubercular, or cancerous, or arthritic, or collagenic. All the tests showed perfectly normal results, but the fingers remained swollen and painful, especially on awakening, after my soul had been in the grip of my unconscious and my body in the chilly grip of night.

I refused to accept degeneration. I would win this race with the necrosis that was gaining on me. Again, I summoned my will, which had always served me so well when I had fixed on a goal. Against death, I had to use action as a drug, to find an outlet for my frustrations. Once more I felt the need to do something difficult, something exceptional, something admirable. Not by plodding but by a brilliant act that would bring relief at once, that would free me at last and put an end to my soul-sickness.

One evening in Ciudad Nueva, we were invited to the home of a West German diplomat. He was young, cultured, spoke French well, and was married to a woman with similar attributes. I had no reason not to accept the invitation. Children shouldn't be made to bear their parents' burdens even if they cannot pick and choose among their heritage: sons of Schiller and of Himmler, of Schumann and of Eichmann, of Hesse and of Höss.

Seated at my table were a man of about sixty and his young wife. Tall, white-haired, with an impressive girth, he ate, talked, and drank heartily. With the second bottle of Moselle, Spanish was abandoned for German. Laughter became coarser and accompanied by elbow prodding; Lanvin ties were loosened and shirts unbuttoned. Everyone began to perspire profusely in spite of the coolness of the evening, which finally let the tropical fragrances filter through.

I couldn't understand very much of what the others were saying or laughing about, but I recognized a few words here and there: *Krieg*, *Juden*, and others. My temperature also climbed, and not because I had had too much to drink. I leaned over to my neighbor and, affecting a detached air, asked what they were talking about and the identity of the swashbuckler who was going on so much. The light-hearted reply left no doubt. He was one of those "little" Nazis for whom a transfer in space had been enough to stop time.

I could feel incredible anger rising in me. I immediately repressed it. If I was going to do something about these bastards, I had to give it some thought and not be content with spitting in the face of a half-drunken underling. I got up from the table and went to vomit.

For a long time the struggle against the Nazis had been part of my fantasies. How often had I walked up Avenue Hoche with my mind galloping against the krauts! Usually I had to stop the charge to cross the Faubourg Saint-Honoré.

This time I knew what I had to do. The solution appeared obvious, natural. I had to kill one, a big one, an important one, not one of these pathetic types on the board of the Colegio Wagner. I had to have one worthy of my anguish. It was all clear now. My mind finally went back to work. I was on familiar ground: an objective, a means, a plan.

At the end of the blind alley, I had found a way out. And also the reason for my punishment: I had escaped the fate of my people, I had abandoned and finally betrayed them. I would avenge them. I would avenge the deaths of the Vel d'Hiv and Chateaubriant, the martyrs of Oradour and of the Struthof,* the gouged-out eyes, the murdered new-born babies, the pregnant mothers whose legs were tied together during labor, the gassed, the saints, and even the kapos. Then and only then would I know peace.

To live I had to kill. But whom?

For several months we had planned to take a vacation in December. Marie-France was enchanted with the idea of an Andean tour—Chimborazo, Cuzco, Machupicchu, Titicaca, Ilimani. Just before we set out, the newspapers gave me the answer I had been seeking: the Supreme Court of Bolivia had just denied the French government's three-year-old request for the extradition of Klaus Altmann, or Barbie, the former Gestapo chief, who had captured and tortured Jean Moulin and who had held sway in Lyon, the city from which my father had never returned.

Thus began a series of coincidences which, for a long time, made me believe that my mission on earth was to kill Klaus Barbie.

*The Vélodrome d'Hiver, known as the Vel d'Hiv, was a bicycle stadium where thousands of Jews—men, women, and children—were held for three days in July 1942 before deportation—the first large-scale round-up in Paris. Chateaubriant is a town in western France where the Nazis murdered twenty-seven prisoners in reprisal for an act of resistance. Oradour-sur-Glane is a village in the Auvergne whose entire population was rounded up by the SS Division Das Reich and burned alive in the village church in reprisal for a series of resistance actions. The Struthof, in Alsace, was the only death camp on French soil.

PART II

The Road to La Paz

Better an end in terror than a terror without end.

—Ferdinand von Schill, Prussian officer who sought and met death in a hopeless struggle against the armies of Napoleon

CHAPTER 5 *Exceptional Services*

Altmann-Barbie was a veteran of the Black Order. He had been in charge of the Gestapo in Lyon when my father was captured. French courts had twice sentenced him to death in absentia. The extradition of a man who was only fraudulently Bolivian had been denied under shocking conditions by a ruling of the court of Sucre, whose mandate had just been terminated by President Hugo Banzer-Suarez. His decision was known but had not yet been implemented when the court, which had taken its time thinking about it, hastened to hand down a ruling, thus rendering a final service to the master of the moment, who could be expected to show his gratitude.

One can get an idea of the spirit behind this decision from a statement made by Altmann's lawyer, Constantino Carrion, to the press: "There is no offense in the Bolivian criminal code entitled 'Crimes against humanity,' the charge against German citizens who defended their country during the Second European War."* This is fairly

El Diario, December 12, 1974.

typical of justice in a part of the world that eagerly consents to be the garbage dump of European history.

No further legal action could be taken against Barbie. He was now free of any legal worries related to his past as a zealous SS officer.

Since no one else seemed in a position to disturb his peaceful existence, I would. To exorcise the spectre of those who had died unarmed; to avenge my father, whom I should have accompanied to Lyon that Monday; to avenge the members of the Resistance who had suffered and died at Barbie's hands. My dual allegiance provided me with a double reason for acting. And perhaps Altmann would help me to answer the question that continued to haunt me—I, who had been unable to take part in the struggle when it was time: Would I have had the honesty to see and the courage to act? He owed me that much! Perhaps, finally, to live in a world of such easy forgetfulness seemed reprehensible to me. Would those stacks of shoes, those piles of eyeglasses, which I still dreamed about—I, who hadn't known them—so quickly join the Albigensians and Saint Bartholomew's Day and other massacres consigned to a paragraph in history textbooks? I would try to interrupt the course of forgetfulness. I would kill Klaus Barbie.

I told my wife about my plan, which she approved enthusiastically. I thought I saw in her eyes a flash of admiration that I hadn't seen for a long time. We made no change in our forthcoming Andean tour; it was just that the trip became a reconnaissance mission.

To leave that country when one is a resident is no small matter. One needs clearance from the tax authorities, which can generally be obtained within forty-eight hours if one knows the right person. But the new president had chosen Christmastime to launch one of those campaigns against corruption which are part of the inauguration rituals. The result was an increase in the price of the clearance and the time it took to get it. All the more so since a great many people wanted to leave the country, while the bureaucrats were already preparing to celebrate Christ's birthday.

In order to qualify as an emergency case, I pretended that my aunt in Lima was dying. But I needed a document to prove it; a telephone call is not tangible. I arranged for someone to send me a telegram from Lima and we received the famous clearance two hours after the plane on which we were scheduled to leave had taken off. Delightful Latin America, where every procedure seems to have built-in complications so that the greatest possible number of citizens will have an opportunity to sell favors! *Gestores* and, in Brazil, *despachentes* are the names given to these unemployed citizens who carry forms obtainable nowhere else, carbons, and even official stamps in their attaché cases. Through discreet redistribution of part of their fees to the officials on whom they depend, they correct inequities in salaries while helping to reduce unemployment and improve the quality of public service.

We had to change planes at Bogotá to get to Lima. I still wonder why the Spaniards chose to establish the capital of their empire in this lowland, which is not even a port, when conquerors usually settle in cooler and less humid altitudes; the Incas had better taste. Nevertheless, I was sensitive neither to Cuzco's charm nor to Machupicchu's majesty. I was already full of my project. The more I thought about it, the more justified it seemed.

But why Barbie rather than Mengele, who did not seem out of reach either in his Paraguayan lair? And on the scale of horror, Mengele, the former head doctor of Auschwitz, the "Angel of Death," the dissecter of twin babies, outweighed even Barbie. I sensed that I had chosen Barbie less because of a link, in truth rather abstract, between him and my father's death than because he happened to be at the meeting point of my two affective clienteles: the Jews and the French.

Mengele was hated only by the Jews and their friends. By killing Barbie I would, of course, avenge my father and the other poorly Frenchified victims of the Affiche Rouge and of so many white ones,* but also Jean Moulin and d'Estienne d'Orves, Maurice Ripoche and l'Abbé Bonpain, Lionel Dubray and Pierre Brossolette. In France, Barbie was hated more as the torturer of Jean Moulin than for his role in the death of the Jewish orphans of Izieu. Jean Moulin, the Prefect of Chartres, steeling himself in the shadow of the "unforgettable and imperishable spire," *was*

---

*L'Affiche Rouge was a triangular, blood-red poster displayed throughout Paris which showed the names and faces of the captured and executed members of a Resistance unit including only men of foreign birth, among them several Jews. Capitalizing on that fact, the poster tried to convey the notion that the Resistance as a whole was made up of foreign criminals.

France; the little Jews were only *in* France. But if a man both Jewish and French avenged the national hero, that would make him a "real" Frenchman. As for the orphans, they would have to be included in the claim to better justify the vengeance: it is defensible and even the rule for an army of occupation to hunt down those who attack it, but to kill children!

After that no Ramass would be able to call me a dirty Jew again. Never again would I hear the rich laughter of the master sergeant who had gone to so much trouble putting together the detail for Christmas duty: "I hope the Fellouzes don't decide to attack that night. They'd find only kikes on guard duty." No captain with a red vest and gold buttons would dare say to me: "Died for France, your documents say, but that's vague. Just how *did* your father die?" in the tone one takes in South America to ask a person of a certain age with a German-sounding name or accent: "Just *when* did you arrive?" Never again would my colonel with the false "de" to his name, who had spent the war as a prisoner in a castle turned fortress among well-bred people, dare to confide: "My comrades tell me that at Suez *those* Jews really did know how to fight." Never again would a certain superior officer, who had used the painters, plumbers, and electricians among his draftees to renovate his apartment in exchange for a week's leave, say to me: "If Dreyfus had been a true patriot and a real soldier, he would have committed suicide even if he was innocent, to avoid splitting the country in two." No aristocrat from Lyon and the High Administration, with whom I had had a professional disagreement, would ask amiably, after having tried first to convince me and then to charm me: "And you, my dear fellow, what province do you come from?" Never again would a certain small-time, penniless lady of the manor, who had taken me in as a boarder, warn me before a luncheon to which she had invited the local priest: "He will surely ask what parish you belong to. I think it would be better to pretend that you are Protestant." Never again would a lady with almost the right address complain to me: "In Bordeaux now the daughters of Jewish merchants dress better than my cousins." Never again would a certain matron known for her good works proclaim in my presence: "Those people didn't really deserve that treatment from the Germans. I said so once to the captain of the Kommandantur at a dinner party in the presence of at least fifteen guests, and I assure you that he trembled in his boots." No ambassador of France presiding over a committee that granted scholarships for the United States would say, when discussing a borderline candidate: "We can't delegate someone with a name like that to represent French youth! Are you sure it is too late to accept more applications? I have a nephew much better than this fellow."

Executing Barbie was the price I would have to pay for the right to be myself at home, to be excused for not having blood that had been shed at Agincourt. I wanted to be finally, truly, "Adopted by the Nation," not just the possessor of a useless card that said I was. My entire being was involved in a last-ditch effort to reconcile the Frenchman and the Jew in me so that I could remain whole. I wanted no more of the marginality or the rejection that are the lot of most Jews in France.

Marginality allows one to be what he is, but he hardly counts for much. It is the solution adopted by second-hand clothes dealers and doctors, lawyers and jewelers, professors, tailors, and journalists—all those who carry their jobs in their heads, their hands, or their pockets, all those who have fled the great institutions, understanding instinctively that in those structures they would be at the mercy of the first du Paty de Clam* who came along. This isn't to say that these people have no power at all, only that they are not "the" Power. They have to shout, write, and argue to make themselves heard.

Rejection is the lot of those who want a fragment of power or just truly to belong. It is not enough to cut oneself off from the foreign body; one must prove oneself through the graft of an above-average supply of nationalism and add to it at every turn. The result is a great stiffness in the soul, which rarely recovers from such an operation.

Then there is a third way, a very narrow one, institutionalized by Vichy in its October 3, 1940, law defining the status of the Jews:

Article 8. By decree taken in the Council of State and duly justified, individual jews who . . . have ren-

*Two for the price of one. The first du Paty de Clam was one of the officers most determined to prove Dreyfus's guilt. His grandson and namesake was a bureaucrat in the Vichy Commissariat on Jewish Affairs.

dered exceptional services to the French State may be exempted from the prohibitions provided for in the present law.

So, if one had held a microphone, a pen, or a machine gun in his hand at the right time in the right place, he could remain himself in all circumstances. That was the circle to which I aspired, without realizing it. The entrance fee was high. I would scrub France's latrines in order to belong; I was going to kill a man in order to be accepted.

Barbie did deserve death, ten thousand times over, but did I deserve to become a murderer? I realized that it was no longer a matter of either finding relief or avenging my father, but of calling for help, of provoking a final speech from Malraux, the man who made Jean Moulin the "Carnot of the Resistance" and whose voice was not yet silent. I wanted a fragment of the glory, of the only real French nobility of the twentieth century, made up of those people who had drawn their swords when needed—and I wasn't one of them.

The local choo-choo from Cuzco to Puno puffed into LaRaya, over two miles high, Indians in second class, tourists in first. We passed the border just before sailing across Lake Titicaca, without anyone's bothering to open a single piece of our luggage. On our way, we saluted the Bolivian navy's only base, which was patiently waiting for the return of its access to the sea. We saw the Islands of the Moon and of the Sun. The Inca on duty was available to those who wanted to photograph him in his reed boat. By evening, we were in La Paz.

The French ambassador, himself a former deportee, explained to me in detail his efforts over the previous three years to have Barbie extradited. He was still very miffed about having failed. No, he didn't know where Barbie was. He didn't have the means to find out, the ambassador said. Did he guess what I had in mind? If so, he didn't let on.

Israel's ambassador told me that his government had had enough problems with the Eichmann matter and that, besides, it would be ill-advised to irritate a country that was still willing to vote in favor of Israel at the United Nations. At any rate, this Barbie matter was primarily a French affair. About Altmann he was a know-little.

It didn't take me long to find out that Barbie was living in Cochabamba. The city's moderate altitude, compared to that of La Paz, was better for his wife, Regina, and visitors there did not go unnoticed. That didn't help me, even if Cochabamba had more oxygen and was more pleasant than La Paz. General de Gaulle spent his one night in Bolivia there during his Latin American tour.

I left Marie-France among the llama foetuses being sold in the market as good-luck charms and set out alone for Cochabamba, where Haim Topol, violin in hand, seemed to wink at me from the billboard advertising the film of *Fiddler on the Roof*.

Barbie lived almost at the end of Avenida Peru in the home of his friend Kremser. I photographed the house from every possible angle. During the whole morning I spent watching it, only an old Indian woman came out. I couldn't stay there forever. I had lunch in a garden restaurant on the edge of town, where there were arbors almost like those in Nogent. Just as my dessert arrived, a group of Europeans, obviously local residents, entered. The owner gave them a warm welcome and seated them three tables away from me. I could hear them speaking a Germanic language that was difficult for me to make out. A white-haired man was seated at the end of the table. Was *he* Barbie?

Any action then was out of the question; Marie-France would surely be arrested as an accomplice. But I had to know what Barbie looked like. I went over to the group and found a pretext for engaging them in conversation. They invited me to sit down. They were Dutchmen who had been in Cochabamba since the war. The white-haired man had met Barbie once at the airport and had refused to shake his hand.

I decided to find photographs of Barbie and try to get a look at him before acting. I was haunted by the idea that I might shoot at the wrong target.

The taxi driver who took me back to the airport used the occasion to point out the high spots. An unwitting humorist, he showed me the prison and told me, in a scandalized tone, that it didn't even have showers. From all points of view, it would be better to do the job in La Paz. I rejoined my wife for a dismal Christmas Eve. We were both deep in our own thoughts, already each one of us alone.

On January 7, Barbie announced that he was going back to La Paz "to resume his activities." What an amusing way of putting it! Under his management the unfortunate Transmaritima Boliviana had come very close to bankruptcy. Actually, he was going to help the Bolivian government in an area he knew better: he was, in effect, a consultant in matters of intelligence—some people even say that was one of the reasons the Bolivians were not eager to extradite him. He knew too much. His return to La Paz suited me: I saw in this new coincidence confirmation of what I had to do. We headed back to Ciudad Nueva.

The route to Barbie led naturally through Paris, to which I returned at the beginning of 1975.

How dear Paris is to someone who believes that he will be deprived of her for a long time! The February sun itself made it hard to leave. The ageless and flowerless Tuileries; the Hotel Meurice, once headquarters of the German army of occupation, now again a shelter for rich lovers. Even the Metro smelled good. Le Marais of my youth, with its old Jewish quarter, had changed very little; my memory of it had erased its grime. All that remained were the scars in the form of plaques and sometimes faded bouquets of flowers hung on the walls of buildings. Rue des Hospitalières-Saint-Gervais, Rue des Nonnains-d'Hyères, Rue Geoffroy-l'Asnier—these street-names, soaked in years, sounded so good.

I did what I had come to do. I contacted a newspaper owned by a man who had committed the dual sin of flirting with Vichy and being overly rich; and I couldn't help smiling at the thought of this old man, who was no more collaborationist than many others but who had paid more dearly, and who was now unintentionally helping me.

Agence Gamma had an excellent collection of photos, almost all of them taken in Lima, which showed a kindly, carefree Barbie having his shoes shined in Plaza San Martín, playing the piano, leafing through magazines. I had them copied and reduced so that I could take them with me everywhere and stamp them on my mind. I also obtained a series of articles that *France-Soir* had devoted to him. I began to know my man. In the archives of the Center of Contemporary Jewish Documentation, I found photocopies of telegrams signed "Barbie," in which he informed his superiors of the capture and deportation of the orphans of Izieu and of eighty-six Jews—among them my father—who were taken on the rue Sainte-Catherine in Lyon on February 9, 1943. I also retrieved a copy of a moving work by l'Amicale des Anciens devoted to the deportation. The photos in that book would strengthen my determination if it wavered. And it did waver a little.

At home again, I wondered if I was on the right track. Strolling aimlessly in my native city, perusing books, seeing friends again, breathing familiar air, I understood that all this was indispensable to me.

In Ciudad Nueva I was suffocating, surrounded by *nouveaux riches* trying to emulate Americans, *anciens riches* emulating Europeans, Europeans who had fled the Allies, the police, or the tax collector, and middle managers turned top managers overnight through expatriation. The Americans from north of the Rio Grande were numerous enough to live in a comfortable ghetto while waiting for their colonial tour of duty or the nationalist squall to come to an end. As for the inhabitants of the *ranchitos* that slide downhill with each heavy rain, they belonged to another world, one with which contacts were difficult and rare. Once I saw a kid stealing mangoes out of my yard with a tin can tied to a long pole. I invited him in, to make it easier for him to get at the fruit, but he thought it was a trap and fled. Another day, my car broke down in a *quebrada*, a fault in the terrain which turns riverbed when it pours. Naturally, the area of greatest flooding coincides with the borders of the shantytown enclave within the rich quarter. It was clear from the hostile stares directed at me that I was considered an intruder, one who profited from the prevailing injustices, and that it would be wise for me to repair my car quickly and alone.

In Paris, I wondered if my plan wasn't suicidal: since I wasn't able to build, I had decided to destroy. Perhaps my project of death would make my rebirth possible. I decided not to tell anyone about it, especially not a very dear friend who was living in New York at the time. It seemed to me that he could only disapprove. Well, through yet another coincidence, he felt the need to pursue me by telephone across the ocean. Finally he reached me at my hotel in Paris. No, he had nothing special to say to me, he just thought we should see each other.

The air network of Latin America resembles the French rail system. It is easier to reach any Latin American capital from New York, or at least Miami, than from any other city, including those in Latin America itself. So I returned by way of New York. Contrary to what I had expected, my friend did not try to dissuade me. "Kill him," he said. "But don't get caught."

Should I try to escape? Wouldn't it be better to face trial? That was one of my dilemmas. If this murder was to take on its full meaning, its perpetrator should not try to evade justice. Since Altmann could not be tried, his murderer would be. The publicity would inform or remind people of what the Nazi regime had been and why the crimes committed in its name were unforgivable, beyond all statutes of limitation, for their wantonness, their unnecessary cruelty, their scope, their institutionalization.

A court would never dare give me a heavy sentence. Bolivia doesn't have a death penalty, and I couldn't care less about a little stint in prison. I even found the idea appealing. I reasoned that veterans of the anti-Hitler crusade would bring pressure to free me on little Bolivia, which was so dependent on the outside world; that France could not allow the person who had avenged the latest occupant of the Pantheon to rot in jail. Even the Soviets could become humanitarians, at little cost; and Kissinger, a Jew who had fled Nazi persecution, was now secretary of state of the country with the most influence in Bolivia.

I imagined that Marie-France was already seeing herself and her three young ones on the cover of *Paris-Match*, at the head of a march for my freedom, flanked by the usual demonstrators. She would be recognized, admired, pitied, and supported wherever she went. I saw her also, perhaps unjustly, finally rid of a husband who oppressed her, free at last.

I returned to Ciudad Nueva in a pensive mood and found my wife entirely devoted to my project. She typed letters to my banks, to my friends, to my colleagues. I had thought of everyone who might be affected by my act. They could be divided into two groups: my friends, who I thought would approve, or at least understand; and the others, those who had slighted me, humiliated me, ignored me, those I would be delighted to thumb my nose at. I signed the letters. All Marie-France would have to do was date them and send them off after the murder.

I took advantage of a trip to Mexico to buy the weapons I would need. There was almost an embarrassment of riches to choose from. The voluble taxi driver had a photo of his sons and a holy picture above the glove compartment. He became friendly in no time and proudly showed me the treasures it contained: a small toolcase, two packages of contraceptives and, hidden behind a rag, a box of fifty cartridges and a 9mm automatic. He was happy to take me to his dealer, who quickly found the short-barreled, five-cartridge revolver I wanted.

That weekend, I went to an isolated corner of the country to practice.

It was Saint-Somebody's day and the hotels were full. Rather than spend the night in my car, I ended up taking a room in one of the local brothels that served as auxiliary hotels with no obligation to sample the tired and sometimes poisonous charms of its residents. Wasn't it the most moral of transactions for a prostitute to lend her bed to someone for the price of a few tricks? The seedy room looked out onto a street where there was a funeral parlor. I could seen the coffins from my second-floor window: some large and padded for rich adults, others small and made of painted wood as if better to emphasize that infant mortality prefers to strike the poor. "Funerarios La Paz": all night the neon sign blinked its message through my jalousies. Was it still another wink of destiny?

In the morning I bought three nice watermelons at the market and went to try out my revolver. I began by shooting at very close range and then moved back little by little so as to determine the maximum distance at which I regularly shot a bullet into the fruit. The pain in my hand was gone.

Some time later, a distant cousin of King Faisal showed me how easy it is to kill a man point blank.

The moment for a journey back in time had arrived. When I returned to Ciudad Nueva, I carefully hid all my hardware in my boots near the bottom of my duffel bag, gambling that customs officials would be too lazy to examine it that far down. I kissed my children, but hardly more warmly than usual. Marie-France accompanied me to the airport in silence, and I set out again on my Andean route.

CHAPTER 6 *Death of a Nazi*

It was night when I arrived at Lima's Jorge Chavez Airport. The line at customs seemed endless. I didn't dare put my bag down. The passenger just in front of me was discovered to have a measuring instrument undeclared on the holy form. He and the customs official argued heatedly. At last the big chief customs officer, who had been alerted, appeared. He began by giving the passenger hell and then berated his own subordinate for good measure. "The ABC of this job is to use judgment," he said. To show what he meant he came over to me:

"Tourist?" he asked.

And without even waiting for a reply, he moved me through with an emphatic gesture:

"Pass, Señor!"

On the train from Cuzco to Puno, I was seated opposite a cultured German tourist who had fought on the Russian front. He spoke French very well and showed no reluctance to reminisce about the war. He couldn't have found a better listener.

"Did you believe in the Nazi ideology?"

"No, of course not; but I wanted my country to win."

"Up to what point did you believe that it would?"

"Until I was wounded in Russia. I did all I could to prolong my convalescence."

I asked him how he felt about a divided Germany.

"It's the price of defeat. . . . But what your Gambetta once said about Alsace-Lorraine, we say of reunification: 'Think of it always but speak of it never.' The day will come when the fact that we are once again powerful will have to be taken into account and our deepest wish fulfilled. If you add up the medals collected by the two Germanies at the last Olympics, you will see the place we hold in the world."

We were a thousand leagues away from the lovely countryside we were crossing. I visited the Islands of the Sun and the Moon again. The Inca was still on duty in his reed boat.

Having entered Bolivia through the back door, I arrived in La Paz that same evening. I wandered around the city's sloping streets prey to the loneliness of my project. A jealous husband had just shot his wife and mother-in-law in the middle of the Prado: I would have some colleagues.

It took me a few days to get to Barbie, posing as a journalist. The next-to-last link in the chain was a North African Jew who had been living in Bolivia for twenty years. I met him in a game-room which one reached by passing through a bank office.

"How do you know Barbie?" I asked.

"I met him at work. He spoke French well, we became buddies. I didn't know who he was. I only found out when I saw his picture in the papers. But that's an old story. We are still buddies."

"Is it easy to reach him?"

"You must be joking! He is always afraid, especially since the Bolivians refused to turn him over to France. He's sure someone's going to get him."

"Who?"

"A Jew, he thinks."

"And how would this Jew find him?"

"I don't know. He could do like you and say he's a newspaperman. Except in his case, it wouldn't be true."

"That's *his* problem. How can I get to see Barbie?"

"Come to the Caravelle tomorrow around ten o'clock. I'll take you."

I asked him if he liked it in La Paz.

"Yes," he said. "It's peaceful here. From what they say, there is less traffic than in Paris."

I spent a restless night. I decided that I would go to my first meeting with Barbie unarmed, simply to see him, to spot any bodyguard he might have, and to find out about his movements.

At ten o'clock on Friday, I was standing in front of the cafe on Calle del Mercado, mouth dry and hands clammy. My guide arrived on time and took me all the way up Avenida Camacho to the La Paz pastry shop, where the

Indian waiters were already having difficulty plowing their way through the crowd of white customers. Seated at a table in the back of the room, I thought of the nightmares in which I tried to cross a tightly packed mass of people who refused to open up and make a path for me. My guide, whose eyes were riveted on the door, gave me a sign when Barbie entered. Still youthful looking, very European, rather small, wearing tie and hat for protection from the equatorial sun, Barbie looked very much like his photos. It took him a long time to reach us because he received a greeting from almost every table he passed. I shook his hand, surprised that I felt no special disgust.

He was not happy to learn that I was a journalist: "The case has been tried and closed. There is nothing more to say about it." Besides, I had heard that he was upset that people to whom he had sold interviews had failed to send him copies. Nevertheless, he sat down beside me and was soon joined by a Croatian and a certain Alex, a Bolivian who was a very much wanted man in his native Hungary. Barbie was clearly the local celebrity; his prestige had been enhanced when he had shouted "Heil Hitler!" at a meeting of La Paz's German colony presided over by a West German diplomat, who had him expelled from the gathering.

The conversation took a turn reminiscent of sidewalk café discussions model 1942. Alex grabbed me by the sleeve:

"The Americans," he said in a pompous tone, "can't drive the whole world crazy forever just because of three million Jews."

Alex's upper denture came loose. He snapped it back in place with a strong jaw movement.

"When I think of that German Jew Kissinger who is making a pile!" added the Croatian, probably one of those Ustachis who had helped Hitler slaughter the Yugoslavs. "Another coffee, please."

I steered the conversation toward Barbie, who showed surprise.

"But why so much hatred on the part of the French? Me, I have nothing against them. My son is married to a Frenchwoman. I have stayed in touch with the veterans of the Charlemagne Division—you know, the French who volunteered to join the Waffen SS. I even took pleasure, a few years ago, in stopping off at Orly Airport."

His Spanish was effortless. He looked at me as though he wanted me to vouch for his good faith. The man was known to be dishonest. I was unable to determine whether he really believed what he was saying, whether he grasped the enormity of it.

I played my role as a journalist, but not a sympathetic one.

"And the torture of members of the Resistance?"

"The French have done much better since in Algeria. What is the name of that general of yours who wrote a book bragging about it?"

His smile was not even ironic.

"And the deportation of the Izieu orphans?"

"That wasn't me, it was Eichmann. I was responsible for the struggle against the Resistance—in other words, against Communism. The anti-Jewish struggle was the work of special commandos who hardly saluted me on arrival and departure."

"Nevertheless, there are many telegrams of arrest signed by you."

"They are false."

I looked at him incredulously. He corrected himself.

"Or else they had me sign them, but I didn't pay attention to what I was signing; there was a lot of bureaucracy, you know. At any rate, I have thousands of friends here."

"And millions of enemies elsewhere."

"They cast stones at us today because we lost the war. The conqueror makes his own law. But why does France blame me for doing my duty as a German officer and not the Frenchmen that she has right there, who were in no way obliged to help us with so much . . . zeal?"

"Who, for example?"

"That I will tell if they continue to annoy me. And then many people will be sorry!"

He was clearly irritated by the nature and precision of my questions. He tried to switch the subject.

"Don't you think there are more serious and more current problems than those of a war that I stopped thinking about the day I turned in my gun? Vietnam, for example. We were the forerunners in the struggle against Bolshevism. Look at where they are now! That would never have happened if the Americans had not made us lose the war. Besides, I prefer the Russians to the Americans. They are more cultured, more intelligent, more courageous. . . ."

"Would you have preferred Russian camps to American camps?"

"No, of course not, but the camps and the purges are the work of the Communists. I said I liked the Russians, not the Communists!"

"Siberia already existed under the czars."

Brief silence. Basically, the only constant in their ideology was anti-Semitism. Nevertheless, none of these Nazis seemed willing to claim or accept any part of the responsibility for the massacre.

Alex, whose denture was clattering tragically, brought us back to the subject of Barbie.

"But Klaus, why are they after you so much? During most of the time you were in Lyon you were only an Obersturmführer."

Barbie was cut to the quick.

"Of course. But I had more power than a general, and in the capital of the part of France that was still resisting! By arresting Jean Moulin, I changed the course of history."

"??"

"Jean Moulin, de Gaulle's man in France, was so intelligent that had he lived it is he and not de Gaulle who would have presided over the destiny of France after our departure. France would probably have become Communist."

Then, changing the subject again: "You realize that the problems the West faces today stem in large part from the fact that the Jews have committed a great injustice by settling on Arab land."

"Would you have preferred that they create their State in Bade-Wurtemberg?"

Embarrassed silence. There is no doubt that he would have preferred no State at all, and no Jews either. But he didn't dare to express his nostalgia for the ovens.

"I'm hungry," he said in French, almost without an accent.

It was 1:30. We walked a little way together on the sunlit Prado. Then the group broke up. Barbie took his leave. A few seconds later, I turned around. He was going up the stairs to the Daiquiri Restaurant. He too turned. Our eyes met for an instant, in spite of the distance. It would be useless to wait for him to come out, and the Daiquiri has several exits.

I was shaken by this encounter, suddenly exhausted by the effort I had made to appear natural and relaxed in the presence of such a run-of-the-mill monster. I slumped onto a bench. What bothered me most was not having felt the flash of hatred I had expected. I had sat next to him. I had looked at him, listened to him, spoken to him, shaken his hand, and it was difficult for me to think that destroying "that" would change much in the world or in my suffering. He seemed utterly despicable, wallowing in his lies and in the smugness of a defeated soldier. But I felt no hatred for him. My frustration went so far beyond him.

Barbie was going away for the weekend and I decided to do likewise. I had learned a little about his schedule for the next few days during our conversation. My best opportunity to act would come on Monday.

I found myself in Santa Cruz, capital of Bolivia's Orient and of its extreme Right, in a brand-new motel by a swimming pool—the ideal setting for someone who would sleep in prison Monday night. There were apparently only foreign guests in the motel: Brazilians, half-colonizers, half-neighbors; Texans seeking oil; Frenchmen seeking markets for their kettles.

Tired of the silence of my tongue and the roar of my thoughts, I spoke to a young American woman—who turned out to be a Bolivian Jew. Her husband, who soon arrived, seemed to be straight out of one of those shtetls that have been wiped off the map of Central and Eastern Europe. Wonderful Diaspora!

I quickly steered the conversation to the subject of the Nazis in the area. I didn't reveal my plans, but I realized that I would have some local sympathizers. I also learned in passing that well-informed Bolivians thought that France would not have gone about the Barbie extradition request very differently if she had wanted it to fail. The French ambassador was hardly popular. His wife was criticized for having her dog cared for in Lima and her teeth in Chicago, or perhaps it was the other way around. Above all, they thought it was a mistake to have posed the Barbie problem in strictly legal terms in a country where the law is trampled on every day and on a continent where one does not extradite: one expels, one delivers a person, one causes him to disappear, according to need, but one does not extradite. Legal language called for a legal response; and France, or certain French officials, many Bolivians said, were not unhappy about a refusal that avoided opening up poorly healed wounds and who knows what painful revelations.

All in all, in silencing Barbie forever I would be doing a favor to those who feared that he would talk. This was a new element in the debate going on within me. Since meeting Barbie, I had been haunted by two questions: Why did I want to kill a man I didn't hate? And why was I totally uninterested in the idea of trying to escape?

The question that came first in logical order quickly seemed subordinate to the second. Barbie was only an instrument. I wanted to kill him because I wanted to be captured and judged. During the short week I had spent in La Paz, I had tried to plan my escape; but when I did, a great lassitude came over me. Where to strike, what escape route to choose, where to get rid of my weapons—these were questions to which I did not seek good answers. I was more interested in capture than in murder. I could already see myself defending my act, accusing my judges. I wanted the whole world to know that I existed, and who I was. I had to reestablish my identity, to show my courage, to be.

Above all, this murder was an appeal. I wanted to be captured because I wanted them to come for me, to take me out of the near-death that is prison. I wanted them to love me. I who was so hard, so alone, so proud of my solitude, even I wanted to be loved like everyone else. This obvious fact, which dawned on me that Sunday by the blue mosaic pool, was for me a revelation of infinite dimensions. Another world opened up. I needed to be loved—I, who believed that I didn't need anyone! That was the most important lesson I learned during this adventure; as the *Guide Michelin* would say of a three-star restaurant, it was worth the trip.

I was unable to telephone Marie-France during the weekend as I had promised. The Bolivian company responsible for international communications operates only on weekdays. So I called her first thing Monday morning. I wanted to tell her that this was the day. I woke her out of a deep sleep. The connection was bad, and at first she didn't recognize my voice. She mumbled. Worried because she hadn't heard from me, she had taken a sleeping pill the night before. As I didn't know that, I thought she was annoyed with me for having disturbed her rest.

I, who was coming here to earn her love, had disturbed her. "Actually," I said to myself bitterly, "you are going to be the king of cuckolds. Your wife will be rid of you; she will have the glory, the bank accounts, and the boyfriends. France will thank you for having silenced Barbie by granting you the right to wear your star with your head high." If I was to follow through to the end, I had to be loved. Was it to my wife, to my mother, or to France that I wanted to present Barbie's head? France was on the other side of the ocean, my mother on the other side of my life, my wife on the other side of love. So why kill Barbie? For the first time it dawned on me that it wasn't my father I had come to avenge.

My wife's voice faded again and we were disconnected. I was more alone than ever. I almost hoped that I wouldn't find Barbie at the spot where I would be waiting for him with death in hand. Nevertheless, caught up in my own momentum, I went through the motions as planned. I took two tranquilizers and got on my way. At 12:30 I was sitting on a bench in the Prado facing the Daiquiri, sufficiently disguised that I wouldn't be recognized. My revolver was hidden under the poncho so dear to tourists. Would he or wouldn't he come?

At 12:50 Barbie-Altmann approached, engaged in a lively conversation with a gray-haired man. The two men stopped at the edge of the sidewalk about three yards from me. On this continent, where nothing turns out as expected, everything was proceeding according to plan.

And now Barbie is there, at my mercy. Rather elegant in his brown suit, his back turned to me, he stands much closer than the watermelons I used for target practice. There are very few people around, and even if one of my bullets should go through him, the risk of harming anyone else is practically nil.

There he stands, the presumed instrument of my liberation, of my rebirth, waiting. That he has his back to me doesn't bother me. It is no more courageous to shoot an unarmed man from the front than from behind. And besides, I can always call out to him or step down from the curb. I would be on him in two strides.

I am very calm. The revolver rests lightly in my lap, under the poncho, my hand on the grip and cylinder. I feel no pity but rather contempt for this man who does not have the courage to face his past.

Will.

All I need is the will.

I can kill Barbie almost without risk. His gray-haired companion is certainly not a bodyguard, and the police in the area have gone to lunch. I know that unfortunate things sometimes happen to guests of Bolivian prisons; they are not all as comfortable as the one at San Pedro, where Barbie was detained—or protected?—for ten months. Nevertheless, I count on the French embassy to make it more difficult for an accident to occur. My sentence, supposing that Bolivia lacks the good sense to expel me, can only be a light one. Moreover, I can always hope for an early release: there will be no lack of pressure on little Bolivia on my account. Perhaps a timely collapse of government, the 184th in a century and a half of independence, will speed things up even more. That is how Régis Debray, writer and teacher of revolution turned practitioner, who had been sentenced to thirty years, was released after having served barely two. In my arrogance, I fear no police, no court, no countervengeance.

I feel both very weak and omnipotent. I feel that a superior force is guiding my steps and my actions. I look at the two men standing in front of me talking. Something now tells me that to kill is not the right solution. "Every murder is a suicide," Elie Wiesel wrote somewhere.

Obviously justice will never be done. The man responsible for the death of some ten thousand men, women, and children, usually in hideous circumstances, cannot be punished for his crimes. What is cutting off the few years remaining to him compared to the deportation to Auschwitz and the death of the forty-one orphans of Izieu, the oldest of whom was thirteen? How can five smooth bullets, which numb the senses in a fraction of a second, compare to the torture of Jean Moulin and of hundreds of others, day after night? What does a quick death mean to a purveyor of slow death? What is death to a man who has worn the uniform with skull and crossbones? No, justice will never be done.

And what if Barbie's true punishment were this eternal flicker of anxiety? Is it living always to look over one's shoulder, to hesitate before going out, to jump whenever the doorbell rings, to fear every public gathering, to mistrust all strangers? Is that the life I want to snuff out?

I let a few minutes pass between Barbie and myself. Eight minutes. Finally, he and his companion shake hands in the European manner, without embracing. Then he crosses the street, goes up the stairs to the Daiquiri, and sits at his usual table near the window. From where I stand, I can sometimes see the back of his head.

I stay where I am for a long moment. I even go up the stairs to the restaurant and watch Barbie through the little glass swinging-door while he is eating. I can still go in and fire.

I leave. I breathe deeply. I tell myself that I could have killed him if I had wanted to, that I intentionally decided not to do so for what seemed to me powerful reasons. I spare. . . .

Actually, I had just inflicted defeat on myself. It was the first, in the area most important to me and probably the only one in which I was vulnerable. Was it to make myself suffer or to cure me? It is not Barbie I killed but myself, the person I had been up to then.

So I did kill a Nazi in La Paz, but not the one I had planned to kill.

My father in his French uniform during the period 1939–40, when France was at war with Germany.

The only picture of father and son together, taken a few months before the former's deportation.

I had a peaceful war.

Foreign and French Jews being inducted by French gendarmes into one of the transit camps before deportation. This photo was taken by the Nazis for an anti-Jewish exhibition but was not used because the Jews didn't look repulsive enough for the purpose. The first civilian on the left (arrow) is presumed to be Joseph Goldberg.

Klaus Barbie, alias Altman: profile of evil.
(*Source: Keystone*)

Jean Moulin, alias Max: face of courage.
(*Source: Roger-Viollet*)

First love: mother and son at the end of the war.

Charles Collenot, the good neighbor who saved our furniture, my skin, and, for a time, my faith in France—being decorated after the war. (*Source: J. Soulet*)

Liberated, or so I thought.

Recovering from rickets among the pines.

Barbie in Lima. (*Source: Agence Gamma*)

"To do in order to be" . . . (*Source:* Le Point

Barbie. These same hands . . .
(*Source: Agence Gamma*)

The only known photograph of the Entebbe hostages under detention. The author, at far right, is translating Idi Amin's words into French. (*Source:* The Voice of Uganda)

Michel Goldberg.
(*Photo: Bert Berinsky*)

PART III

"If I Forget Thee..."

The importance of failure is crucial . . . if one has not understood this secret . . . one has understood nothing and glory is futile.

—Jean Cocteau, *Opium*

CHAPTER 7 *Non-Crime and Punishment*

When I awoke the next day the pain in my right hand had worsened. It had totally disappeared during my Andean hunt, but it had now returned and spread to my thumb, making it hard to exert any pressure with my hand. Bending my fingers, turning a key, opening a tin can, shaking a hand, even holding a pen caused pain that was difficult to bear.

I looked at my thumb, my index finger, and my middle finger. What symbols! But which symbol was involved now? *Yad*, the hand, which also means "memorial" in Hebrew, this right hand is so loaded with meaning that one can lose oneself in it. The fingers, indispensable for handling a gun, are also the fingers of power, of the "hand of justice." The middle finger is a sexual symbol. (General Banzer, who knew better, asked his followers to raise their index fingers as a salute to him.) But what haunted me most of all was the biblical phrase, "If I forget thee, O Jerusalem, let my right hand forget her cunning. . . ." Which was the message? Was I guilty of having forgotten

Jerusalem? If one listens to voices too much, doesn't one end up hearing them?

I returned to Ciudad Nueva. My wife's disappointment was evident. Her husband was back; her hero had failed to bag his prey. He was just an ordinary human being pushing forty, losing his hair, and developing a pot belly. He was no longer worthy of crushing her with his arrogance and his body.

I was grateful to her for having left me free to plan my project. But I had the right to give it up. If she was to continue to bear her miseries with me, she had to admire me. Her disappointment clearly showed that she was no longer attached to me, and I believed that I was no longer attached to her. So I proposed a separation, the true dimensions of which I in no way measured. She hastened to accept. I entered on the path of divorce as I had on that of marriage; headlong and heart-short.

Came the time of accidents, public and private, moving and still. While I was waiting for a light to change on La Principal, Ciudad Nueva's main street, one of the numerous motorcycle messengers who zigzag between lanes smashed into the rear of my station wagon. Blood and a whitish liquid oozed from his nose. I put him in the back of the car and waited for the police. The law is very explicit: it is forbidden to move vehicles involved in an accident before the police arrive. Whether one is in the middle of a superhighway, under a tropical downpour or a bludgeon-sun, one must wait for "the authorities."

Twenty minutes later, neither the police nor an ambulance had arrived. On the other hand, I began to be in serious need of protection. All around me clusters of motorcyclists brandishing chains or wrenches were urging me to take their colleague to the hospital. I agreed silently with them that it was not worth letting this poor fellow lose blood, and perhaps more, just out of respect for the letter of a law. I grabbed a witness and took the injured man to the nearest hospital.

An hour later, with tubes coming out of his nose, my reclining cyclist, who had not lost his bearings despite a fractured skull, informed me that I was in the wrong for having moved my car and that he was going to claim I had knocked him over unless I was "understanding."

After phoning my lawyer, I went back to the bedside of the injured man and told him that if he did not sign a discharge of responsibility on the spot, I would tell the hospital that I would not pay his bill and they would throw him out on the street. With a few sighs of adieu to the lifelong income he had already spent in his imagination, he signed and I paid for his stay at the hospital. My insurance company refused to reimburse me: I shouldn't have moved my vehicle.

Retrospective curiosity led me to ask my lawyer what, in my place, he would have done to stand up to the pack of motorcyclists. He simply raised his coattail; protruding from his belt was the grip of a revolver.

"All you had to do was ask me to get you a gun license."

Lost in my Andean peaks, I had not realized that the

murder of Barbie would have preceded by only three weeks the thirtieth anniversary of the liberation of the camps. France had planned to commemorate it with special solemnity. Even the time of the murder had been well chosen, unknowingly!

Back in Paris that Sunday, before the Monument to the Unknown Jewish Martyr on Rue Geoffroy-l'Asnier, in the heart of Le Marais, I heard the hopeless chants of Jews mourning their six million dead. For the first time in a long while I let my tears flow.

A few feet away, in the Ile de la Cité's prowlike crypt, official France was celebrating the memory of its two hundred thousand deportees who never returned. In principle, my father was accounted for on both sides, so I went. But the crypt was protected by policemen in dress uniform and a black wall of official cars. I couldn't enter. One had to show a white card. I hadn't paid enough.

Young ambassadors of countries born after the war walked solemnly to the ceremony, which would probably bore them, while I was excluded. I beat a retreat by way of the Pont Saint-Louis, turned back to take a last look at the island of my city, dominated by its church, and I then felt how much Notre-Dame, Our Lady, was theirs.

I obtained a leave of absence from the bank. Depression among the upper echelons was as much a part of corporate life as secretarial pregnancies and computer breakdowns. Michel Cojot, Director for Spanish America, was replaced in Ciudad Nueva. I repatriated my furniture, and Marie-France settled down in it with the children.

I have said little about the children up to now, but they did exist, three of them. I didn't pay much attention to them except to encourage the boys to outdo themselves. I spoke at them, checked their schoolwork, and gave them a spanking from time to time for good measure. Sometimes they amused me, as when I found them up on the roof because the radio had warned of an earthquake. At other times they annoyed me—for example, when the oldest threw a ball into the school's loudspeaker to dislodge a swarm of wasps and came home disfigured by their stings. But outward signs of love, none at all. I wanted good soldiers. As for the girl, she was still too small to seem more to me than a wobbling, noisy, dirty digestive tube.

Suddenly I amputated them from me and felt pain of an unknown nature. I, who had always been an early riser, could no longer get out of bed; my limbs felt heavy and painful. Every movement was a problem. Nothing had meaning. Everything was an effort and all effort was futile. Could it be that I, who had always shrugged my shoulders on hearing of other people's "depression," was myself afflicted? I had to face facts. I no longer wanted to live or to give life.

The only time I felt life flow in me was on weekends when I saw my children. Until then, "seeing" someone had implied that I had business with him. With my children it was different. It was enough for us to be together. I discovered how much I needed them.

Today I know that I owe my life to my children. But for them I would have returned to La Paz to seek, no longer glory or redemption, but death by closing the door on a world that did not want me. I hesitated a long time. I grew a heavy moustache—Barbie had known me clean-shaven—in case I should decide that killing him was my only way out. Only my children still held me back.

I found myself alone precisely when I was beginning to understand what love is. It was the absence of love that had led me to the brink of murder and suicide. The death I was now suffering was worse than death because it had left me alive. I was a living dead man. Everything in me wilted. Death had entered me by the path where life exits. Oh, the lewd walls of my Paris hotel pierced by the cries of a woman bursting with pleasure! I looked at the insipid wallpaper in a daze. Was it my failure to kill Barbie that had earned me this punishment?

Before, I had never had enough time. Now I didn't know what to do with it. I was confused. I left Paris because the thought that my children were only a few minutes away was unbearable. But they were so accustomed to seeing me leave! My daughter would wish me a good trip if I left the house to buy a newspaper.

I wandered to Madrid, where I stayed a long while. I wrote my children letters that I never sent. In the early hours of the morning, when sleep abandoned me, I would take the pen in my painful hand and try to explain to them why the man and the woman who had come together to give them life were separating after thirteen years; why daddy and mommy had decided to inflict the worst on them, to turn their world upside down, to make them suffer.

"Even when you are laughing, you are suffering," I wrote them. "And you will suffer even more. You, Guillaume, even though you are plucky and eleven, you ache and already understand. How sad you were that Christmas Eve when everything was there—the tree, the candles, the mistletoe, the snow—everything except mommy.

"You, Laurent, Laurent-Joseph, the first to revive my father's given name, you are suffering, too, but you don't know it yet. That is worse. Your innermost being will probably be shaken because one day during your childhood the ground under you gave way. The love on which you built yourself, the love that gave you wings and laughter, the love that you took for granted like air, sun, or water, you are learning that this is fragile and perishable. And if later you happen to doubt yourself or your other, it may be because we betrayed you at the age of reason. You take comfort in the fact that you have your mother to yourself. I pray to heaven that you never feel guilty about it.

"And you, my little Aviva, you for whom Barbie is the name of a doll, you with whom I follow the same path and probably make the same mistakes as my mother with me, you whose Hebrew name is equivalent to your circumcision and my identity, you, the first one I knowingly loved, you who see your mother with a stranger, you who no longer know where to love, what can you understand? When you are with mommy, there is no daddy, and when you are with daddy, mommy is not there. To hear your joyful transformation of the *Chant des Partisans*—'Ami, entends-tu le velours des corbeaux sur la plaine,'*—who could say that you are in pain?

"Three children suffering. That's no small matter. At the moment it is everything to me. And it is so hard for me to write to you. . . ."

My hand hurt, but not as much as my heart. I wanted to tell them, to explain, but I didn't know where to begin. I became entangled in chronology, modesty, shame, and pain. . . .

Then the divorce came. It was I who had taken the initiative; nevertheless, I ended up in the position of feeling that my wife had abandoned me. Mine had been a pedestal marriage. I was the statue and Marie-France the base, inferior by nature. But when the pedestal happened to be missing, the statue collapsed. I had put the cord around my neck and contemptuously kicked away the stool on which I was perched. And I was surprised to find myself overcome by death.

I realized that I was much more attached to Marie-France than I had thought. She remained joined to me in a thousand places, which became as many wounds. We had ritually granted each other freedom, yet I was jealous. It was the vengeance of all those popular songs that I had

*"*Ami, entends-tu le vol lourd des corbeaux sur la plaine*" ("Friend, do you hear the heavy flight of the crows [Krauts] on the plain") is the first line of the Anthem of the Resistance. Aviva's version substituted *velours* ("velvet") for the ominous image.

disdained so much, of all the films that had bored me, of all the "love stories" that I had refused to read. Barbara Cartland knew much more about life than I did.

Our marriage had been a failure, but we decided to try to make our divorce a success. Undoubtedly we still loved each other. On the whole, everything came off gracefully.

The little man my wife had engaged as her lawyer didn't understand that the future ex-spouses didn't want to tear each other apart. How could he demonstrate his skill if there was no fight? How would he be avenged for having to wear lifts in his shoes if he couldn't fight? He was small the way some people are Jewish; he tried to hide it. From this came a formidable aggressiveness which he mobilized against his clients' adversaries. I had to put up with his arm waving, his "my client," and his bad breath.

I relinquished the custody of my children without a fight. I thus cheapened myself in their eyes. Father was no longer God. They could appeal my decisions, they could leave the paternal sphere. I had either not wanted or not known how to hold on to the woman my children loved; silently they reproached me for it; they also rejoiced, because their big rival had been cast aside. My image was tarnished, but so was theirs since they looked at themselves in my streaked mirror. I had to come to terms with them. They felt an increase in status, but has anyone ever seen children enhanced by their father's decline? I had to resist my daughter's flirtatiousness, tempting as it was, so that she would be able to love another later.

One country morning, I woke up feeling a need to pray. Whether it was a childhood memory, my daughter's prattle, or the scent of the mist lazying over the river, I wanted a church—not a lofty, cold dwelling of the God of thunder, but a cottage with moss on the outside and the smell of wood on the inside. I put on my rubber boots, took my daughter in my arms, and went to the village. I was a little ashamed, but I was alone with this other self who was my link to life. I pushed the door open and, a little reluctant to perform a gesture from my childhood, I let my fingers dip into the font. Aviva burst out laughing:

"Splash, papa!"

She was so happy to catch me in the very act of putting my hand in the soup.

My children learned where to strike me, and they did so indiscriminately, simply to test their new power. "Mommy's friend," one said, "loves me more than you do, he lets me have all the candy I want." Or: "If my sister goes to you next weekend, I'm not coming."

I had suffered so much from not having a father, and now I was losing my children! No longer did they spontaneously show me their notebooks; their presence became precarious, my stamp on them lighter—and I knew what that would cost them later. Even the French national railways denied me the fare reduction to which parents of three or more children are entitled. I began to think longingly of the rabbinical divorce law which gives custody of boys to the father after early childhood. I had divorced at the wrong time and in the wrong place.

Women, these Jews, are evening the score with men. Preying mantises, with their sugar-coated Pill they are taking revenge for their mothers' submissiveness. My wife managed to combine equality and dependence, freedom and motherhood. I was at liberty to go anywhere I wanted, but at the price of my children. I, who had wandered so much, now lost my freedom of movement.

I caught myself trying to buy my children with gifts that were a little too expensive or not truly justified, using the only power I had left: money. Paltry power! Vulnerable to time as to wind, illusory reducer of anguish, hidden and omnipresent, coveted and despised like a woman's sex, cheap or generous—in the end of ends, money is only emptiness. What is important is what is around it. The investor is always paid in kind. If he invests love, he can receive love; if he invests money, he can receive money. But love that is bought and money that is loved are forgeries punishable by loneliness.

And I knew loneliness. Not the pleasant, fruitful solitude one chooses, but the loneliness one endures, that of Sunday dinner out of a can. The telephone that used to ring so often now was silent. At night, I would wake with a start, and it was an effort for me not to believe that I heard a child crying or that I didn't have to get up to listen for the reassuring sound of breathing.

Hotels, laundromats, furniture storage, empty love affairs. I preferred to see bad films; that way I didn't suffer from not being able to share them. I was a bachelor again, but a little old, a tall midget. I met people in worse distress than I. "Michel, can I spend the night with you? My husband is at our place with a woman and he put me out. Please. I don't have the courage to go to a hotel."

Needing help, I learned to help others without expecting anything in return. My passing affairs were with other cripples. All we had to share was our suffering. Wounded on the same battlefield, each of us helped bandage the other with silent tears.

I was tempted to go to La Paz again. Then I realized what a trap I had set for myself. Not having killed Barbie was perceived as a major failure by my unconscious, but at least there was now a crack in my shell. Killing him would undoubtedly have been an even greater error. I had a choice of scenarios. The most likely was that the murder would have strengthened my feeling of legitimacy, of particularity, of loftiness—my way of not being. It was an act for which there was so much justification, it was so easy to defend—justice over law, the civilized world over the racist core of South America, history over geography, the son to the rescue of the father, the Jew to the rescue of the Frenchman, the intellectual who acts out, the successful executive who abandons all to track crime to the ends of the world, the son of France driven to carry out the sentence of her courts. How could I become myself weighed down by so many clichés? Imprisoned by the image of myself as the lone avenger, how many years would it have taken me to question my act, and above all myself? Would it have been enough to kill Barbie? After him, wouldn't it have been necessary to kill others, and still others? Would I have found the automatic and universal virility to which I aspired? And what trouble would my children have known, overwhelmed as they would have been by a hero-father distant even when he was close?

No. If I really wanted to use Barbie for revenge, I had to strike him down anonymously, without getting caught. Perhaps then I would be able to rebuild my ego on his corpse. It was enough that *I* would know.

If it was justice I wanted, if I wanted to force France to look at her entire past, I had to kidnap Barbie and take him to French Guyana so that he could be judged in France, in person. I sometimes became excited about this plan, now that I no longer had the desire to destroy. Through the chink in the wall of my portable prison, I caught a glimpse of a world different from the one I had known before. The fish that had been out of water for so long was finally returning to its element. If the human law was love, I preferred to aim straight for the pocket rather than bounce off the side-wall of glory. I no longer had the wish to kill. I wanted to love at last. But how does one go about it?

CHAPTER 8 *Back to the Wall*

This hesitation I had felt so often—on the verge of murder, marriage, divorce, or Israel—this means of prolonging my suffering, seemed to me a major weakness. I now encountered in myself the indecisiveness that Michel Cojot had so often criticized in his superiors and colleagues, and it was all the stronger because the railings that confine but protect so many of my half-brothers had long since disappeared. I was at my best only in situations in which there was neither time to hesitate nor the possibility of delaying a decision.

For a long time I had thus postponed my visit to Israel. I knew Beirut, Teheran, Cairo, Katmandu, but not Jerusalem. I had visited pagodas, mosques, pyramids, cathedrals, Baalbek, and Swayambuna, but I had not entered the Temple. Probably in some confused way I realized that I could not do so as a mere visitor; I feared that I would discover the ghetto and that I might feel like a stranger there, maybe even hostile. Of course I justified my behavior with all sorts of reasoned, reasonable reasons, but as time went on I became less successful at deceiving myself.

I admired the epic of these people who had rebuilt a country for the survivors of the camps, the exiles from everywhere: I even helped with word and deed, but from the outside. Israel was not me. Nevertheless, I knew that there was something for me there, a little bit of me, perhaps even a member of my father's family who had miraculously reached the country and of whom I could be proud.

Before our marriage, I had said to my future wife: "One day there will be war between Israel and the Arab countries. When that day comes, don't try to stop me from going to fight." Solidarity in battle and in death; it was the only solidarity I knew.

Today most of the world has forgotten the threats hurled against Israel during the long weeks preceding the Six Day War and how much in earnest they sounded, like not-so-hollow echoes of the Final Solution.

Israel did not need volunteers, but the threat of a resumption of genocide was enough to wake something within me. I was relieved by the brilliant victory. I even took secret pride in it and felt just a little envious that it had been achieved without me. I had been born too late for the just struggle and I was too far away from this one. Was I condemned to be an onlooker of history all my life?

In June 1967, while the Israeli army was savoring its fresh victory, the reunited city, the capture of the Golan, and the reconquest of the Sinai, I was ensconced in a plush-lined barber's chair on the Avenue des Ternes. Some people risked their lives to take the Old City without damaging it; I was risking a cut through some barber's clumsiness. In the chair next to me a talkative customer filled the room with his comments. Israel was in the news:

"Those Jews over there," he began with conviction. "They aren't like the ones here! They really kicked the shit out of those wogs!"

As low a blow as it was, the remark stung. It united Jews and Arabs in the same anti-Semitism. Thus the Promised Land, which did not mind one more miracle, transformed the short, swarthy, cowardly, money-grubbing parasites of the poor sections of large cities into tall, blond men of the earth displaying selfless courage with gun and sickle alike.

Was Israel the Prussia of the Near East, an anti-Semitic state, the land of my ancestors, a land to live or to die for? I had to find out.

Here I was at the foot of the majestic, revered, and silent Wall off which men bounce words addressed to God. In the shadow of this eternal Wall between whose stones mortals slip their perishable requests, the faithful—bearded men with long sidelocks, children, old people—rocked, piously chanting with all their being. I looked at them avidly. Here was a man wearing a fur hat in spite of the heat, there one dressed in black and white, here one with his eyes closed under his broad-rimmed hat. Were these my brothers? Were these the invincible warriors? I felt more ill-at-ease than in a pagoda, much more so than at church. With the cardboard yarmulke ready to fly off my head, I felt like a stranger; worse, like a voyeur.

There was no reason for me to force myself to remain there. If I had, I would have done too much honor to Pouzin-Coffin* and his ilk. I left the area and quickly found myself in Jerusalem's French ghetto.

Yes, there they were, united by *Phèdre* and rillettes du Mans, by *Boubouroche* and Ste. Mère Eglise, to all appearances exactly like their brothers of the XIth Arrondissement and even of the XVIth, of Roanne, Oran, Abbeville, or Ferryville. And yet they were different: they were less Jewish. Admittedly, they observed Hanukkah and not Christmas, worked on Sundays, spread a cloth on the table on Friday evenings, and even went to services occasionally. Nevertheless, in this Jewish world they had shed the scabs of a minority. They could bad-mouth the rabbis to their heart's content, they could mock the Hassidim without being traitors, and they could see Arabs humiliated without identifying with them. They were home.

Had we suffered so much just so that Jews could no longer be Jews? To allow a Jew to be as stupid, as dishonest, and as corrupt as anyone else without fear of giving a bad name to his coreligionists? To be no longer only a

---

*Author of a book awarded a prize by the Académie Française in 1939 as "one of the two best works of ethical and educational literature for youth." It describes those who crowd to the Wailing Wall thus: "Suspicious looks, inscrutable faces . . . with their backs turned to Calvary, which would be their salvation. Didn't the deicide people have a duty to understand and expiate their sin?" *Le plus beau des voyages,* 4th ed. (Paris: A. Reynaud), p. 121.

guest; to be able to eat with his fingers, put his feet on the table, and belch to his stomach's content?

What was Jewish about these tanned sabras? They had rejected the given and even the family names of the Diaspora. They had lost the languages and sometimes even the linguistic ability.

To them the stories of Jews turned into bars of soap seemed so remote, so foreign. So much the better for them, so much the worse for me.

In the line ahead of me, a beautiful woman handed her French passport to a young blond customs officer, who leafed through it warily.

"Are you Jewish?" he asked.

"Don't you see, my name is Frank, like Anne."

"Like who?"

How the devil does one say "Ramass" in Hebrew?

I had just left Beersheba by the truck route, which is empty at this hour, when the light is overwhelming. I should be in Tel Aviv in two hours. Now, I admit that I did not come to a full stop at the intersection of the eucalyptus-lined highway. The desert was flat, and I could see the road clear as far as the horizon. From the shadow of a eucalyptus tree emerged a policeman who stopped me and proceeded to write out a ticket. I argued. It was obvious that I was a foreigner. He looked at me sternly:

"If you don't like it here, you can go back where you came from."

I was right back where I started. I motioned to him to continue writing the ticket.

Poor little Jew, why is there no place for you on earth? In Israel they make you an Aryan, elsewhere they oblige you to go underground or to fly away, Chagall-like; only accession to the universal allows you to place your feet on the ground. Little Jew, whom everyone expects to be great or to disappear, were your values all that contemptible, was your nose that repulsive? Were you too rich or too dirty, too intelligent or too much to the left or too much elsewhere, too mysterious or too brilliant? They built you museums and gave you prizes to exonerate themselves, but who ever felt at home in a museum?

You don't like borders or uniforms or official stamps. You have seen so many flags, heard so many songs, made so many requests, filled out so many forms, presented so many affidavits. The massacre of your European brothers earned you a twenty-year respite, but after that, what? Is there no place for you except in the great cemetery? Is the past your future?

Tired of these questions, the thirteenth tribe had returned to the fold to play again the cruel game of mortal nations.

Israel is a beautiful land, part Provence, part Hoggar, but is it mine? Men and women with numbered forearms weigh oranges. Jews who look like Arabs mount guard around this island. These Jews of the sun and of falafel, of the loud verbs and colorful adjectives, are they mine?

A blend of America and the Levant, of unearthed history

110

and buried present, a land where one looks four thousand years back but not six months ahead, a land fertilized by six million dead and three million living, a people deafened by twenty centuries of screams, a suicidal people so attached to life. A people identified through its mothers and rejected by its neighbors. An "elite people," as de Gaulle had it, but, contrary to his words, so unsure of itself. I am *in* it; am I *of* it?

I finally found my Polish-born "cousin" in a kibbutz. He spoke Hebrew, Polish, German, Yiddish. I spoke none of these languages. We had to resort to sign language, smiles, chance interpreters. It turned out that I had the ears, the laughter, or the walk of people I had never even heard of.

As for my cousin, he was radiant with the certainty of having made the right choice. He had killed mosquitoes in Palestine, chased Germans in Libya and Italy, been wounded in the leg by the British—in short, he had fought at Agincourt. In the egalitarian society of the kibbutz he was an aristocrat. Limping for a just cause, he had the almost exclusive use of an automobile—unheard-of luxury—and the only shaded parking space. In the wake of David Gryn, who became Ben-Gurion, my Goldberg had Hebraicized his name. There were no more Goldberg-Mohicans.

He was my cousin; but was he my brother? He didn't understand me, but he liked me. His children spoke only Hebrew and had never been out of the country. They had been born on the kibbutz, and it is there that they wanted to die. Their horizon was limited by cypresses. They were my country cousins!

I had taken my elder son to Israel with me. First proof of my fertility, fragile hope of my eternity, weakened link in the chain at the age when the Jewish boy—he was only half-Jewish—becomes a man, a goy to the rabbis and burning material to the Nazis, he seemed so solid, this other me for whom everything was still possible. . . .

It was my hope that this trip of two men, linked by the same woman who now separated us, would bring us even closer together. I wanted him to discover his roots through the soil and not, like his father, through the head. I wanted him to find brothers in laughter and not in tears. No doubt I also wanted to stamp this son with my personal seal, he whom I was losing to both time and mother. From the defenders of Masada to the attackers of Acre, from the frenzies of Sodom to the folly of Europe, which was evident everywhere here, we were partners in building up a stock of common history. Having been deprived of a father, I saw to it that my son received a double helping, at the risk of causing him indigestion. He absorbed everything—the geography, the exotic sights and smells, the hummus, the language, the sun. I was happy that he did, and I didn't really try to find out why.

My hand was still hurting, even in Jerusalem. The

medical sachem was learned enough to admit his ignorance. All the tests were negative.

"What would you do in my place?" I asked him.

He shook his handsome crown of white hair à la Ben-Gurion.

"On the road from Beersheba to Gaza there is a village called Netivot," he said. "In this village lives a very old rabbi, from Oran, I believe, or maybe Morocco. They say that he has cured many people given up by the doctors. Go to see him. At any rate, that part of the Negev is worth seeing."

"Is he a rabbi, a doctor, or a healer?"

"A little of everything at once. What have you got to lose?"

At ten o'clock in the morning it was as warm as high noon. The few passersby crept along the walls in the last shadows. Only children, flies, and donkeys ventured out into the sun. I went into a soft-drink merchant's to ask for the rabbi's address. I found a crowd of people speaking three or four languages all at once, all with an accent.

"It is the second street on the left," I was told. "You can't miss it. But you need an empty bottle."

"A bottle? What for?"

"He will tell you. You need one."

"Do you sell them?" I asked the merchant.

He straightened up, cinched up his shorts, which were too big, and assumed the air of Napoleon on the evening following his Jena victory:

"Only full ones," he said.

With my bottle of Tempo in hand, I found the rabbi's house and joined the small crowd that was spilling over the stairway into the bright sunlight. Men, women, children, old people, young people, all had their bottles. I went over to a woman who spoke French. She told me that some of the people were there on their third or fourth visits.

"What does he do?" I asked.

"He is wonderful. He cured an eighteen-year-old girl who was lost. So she married him."

"How old is he?"

"No one knows exactly, but surely more than a hundred."

Again I asked what he did.

"He cures."

"But how?"

"What do you mean, how? That's his secret."

"Did he cure you?"

"I was unable to have children and my mother-in-law cursed me. Now look." She showed me her rounded stomach.

"Then why have you come back?"

"So that my son will be tall and strong."

"Because he also guaranteed you a boy?"

"That's what I asked him for. But, you know, for it to work you have to believe."

I was in Placebo City, a distant suburb of Lourdes. Hope gave way to curiosity.

Finally, I was permitted to enter a waiting room where two or three women offered drinks of lukewarm water with a half-drop of syrup. Then a young man wearing a black jacket and hat led me into the holy of holies.

Ensconced in an armchair, dozing, was a man so old, so thin that it seemed a miracle he was still alive. All around him were little statues, fans, goblets with twisted stems, colored glasses, a silver-plated pie cutter, an elaborate china inkpot—so many offerings from those to whom he had given relief.

The man who had introduced me asked what was wrong. I showed him my right hand. Without waiting for the end of my explanation, he asked for my name and my father's. He repeated this information into the rabbi's ear. Then he placed his own ear so close to the centenarian's mouth that I couldn't see the old man's lips move.

Finally the young man straightened up:

"The rabbi says that you must respect the Sabbath and that you must fill your bottle with water from the faucet outside this house and drink only that. When the bottle is half empty, fill it with any other water, and so on indefinitely."

The man of science had referred me to the man of God, who had referred me back to myself.

CHAPTER 9

*Psychodrama
at Entebbe*

Ben Gurion Airport is an Occidental bazaar. The crowd
tried to make a path among the baggage carts, the pillars,
and the barriers under the watchful eyes of young women
in khaki and young soldiers in tourist uniform, the only
persons there who were not bustling about. Questioning
was serious and luggage was carefully searched, regardless
of the airline. Woe betide anyone who could not convince
the officials that he was harmless: his alarm clock would
be dismantled, the heels of his shoes probed, his camera
opened, his can of shaving cream tested, the cake for Aunt
Rachel, wrapped so carefully the night before, reduced to
crumbs. In this great game of cops and robbers, too often
synonymous with public administration, the Jews had
become cops; but they were in a strong position, having
confronted almost all the other cops in the world. Nevertheless, it all went rather smoothly because everyone coop-
erated and approved of the reasons for the controls. There
were burning memories: the Olympic Games, Maalot—
even here, where three Japanese had wounded or killed

some eighty Puerto Rican pilgrims they had mistaken for children of Israel.

My son and I settled down in the Air France Jumbo. I had tried unsuccessfully to change our reservations to El-Al, which seemed to offer better security. But after this heavy dose of the East it was a pleasure to go back to the language, the elegant restraint of the stewardesses' uniforms, and even the food tray. I had made so many trips to the four corners of the world that Air France had just admitted me into one of its clubs for frequent travelers, whose members receive "service-plus."

On the plane, I wrote a probably useless professional memorandum and then gave Guillaume an exercise in spelling by dictating a vaguely humorous piece on the joys of air travel. We were surrounded by brawling brats, a woman who spilled over her seat on both sides, and a couple of retired Americans.

We made a landing at Athens, where the Americans left us. I was a little surprised at this stop: it had not been announced, perhaps because it was the last time this flight would be required to make it. The airline was finally to give in to the pleas of the crews, who dreaded this airport, well known for its laxity. Either as a matter of prudence or to save time, it was suggested that we stay on board. Once the exchange of passengers had been completed, the huge Franco-German aircraft rose under the thrust of its American engines.

We were directly over Corfu, just above Albert Cohen's,* when I heard a shout and saw a man, bent over, running toward the front of the plane. Worried, the passengers looked up. The rumor that there was a fire spread without smoke or flame; then we saw passengers and stewards, flowing back from the front with their arms raised. One of the stewardesses, pale and nervously waving her hands to calm us, said in a barely audible voice: "It's nothing, we are talking to them."

Two Arabs who could have been Jews and one young Western woman with gun and grenade in hand yelled at them in heavily accented English:

"Sitonzeflor! Sitonzeflor!"

An old Jew sprung up indignantly and spoke as though he was at a meeting of the Bund: a blow to the head from the barrel of a gun made him shut up and sit down all at once. The takeover had been swift and neat. Che Guevara would have been pleased with his flock. We heard the voice of our new "captain" explaining that the plane had been rebaptized *Haifa* and that no harm would come to us if we behaved ourselves. On the other hand . . .

A succession of basic operations followed. First, separate those who were potentially dangerous from the others. Guillaume went to sit next to an Israeli woman of French origin. It was the only time I saw a look of distress on his face. He had become a little boy again, my little boy. Rationally, I was sorry that I had dragged him into an

*Cohen wrote several major novels in French *(Solal, Belle du Seigneur)* which have not yet been translated into English. Born in Corfu in 1895, he died in Geneva in 1981.

119

adventure which could cost him his life; but secretly I was happy that he was with me and I with him. I thought of the father whom I had not accompanied.

We had to submit to a search and hand over anything that could be used as a weapon. Guillaume turned to me with a questioning look: should he surrender the beloved Swiss army knife that he always wore chained to his trousers, much to his mother's annoyance? I nodded in the affirmative, and with the solemnity appropriate to the magnitude of the sacrifice, he added it to the little pile of pocket knives, nail files, knitting needles, and other engines of death that had escaped Israeli vigilance. After the weapons, identification papers—all identification papers; the stewardesses collected passports, driver's licenses, Social Security cards, and God knows what else in plastic bags.

We were supposed to remain silent and keep hands on head. Both of these rules were quickly broken. Time was heavy and so were bladders. A system of permissions worthy of an old-fashioned elementary school was instituted: there were two hundred and sixty-one of us, and we were allowed to use only the two lavatories at the rear of the plane. Returning from the toilet, Guillaume whispered to me:

"I threw away my Star. You'd better do the same."

Again the Star! He had insisted that I buy him a Star of David in the Old City of Jerusalem; mine, the first I had ever worn, had been given to me the night before by the woman for whom I had stayed in Israel an extra day, and I had bought the chain at the airport in the morning. I refused to throw away this dual symbol.

A few old women began to moan louder and louder; one of them, the one who spilled over her seat, wiped her face with a cloth of dubious cleanliness. A very nervous Jew with a yarmulke, the dream of anti-Semites, provoked suspicion or contempt from the young German woman by his frequent requests to go to the lavatory.

There she was in the aisle, a fragmentation grenade, pin out, in her left hand, an automatic pistol, hammer up, in the other. She had the unappealing face of a bookworm; metal-rimmed glasses, plain suit, blue stockings—everything about her was rigid. Still, in the heat of the action, two buttons of her blouse had come undone, allowing a glimpse of breasts primly encased in a rather feminine brassiere. Perhaps to change the subject, the passenger closest to her tapped her on the hip and indicated with his finger that her blouse was gaping. She couldn't repress a smile and tried to adjust the blouse without letting go of her weapons. A little song about the "Tetons of the Teuton" came to my mind. I couldn't help thinking that if she dropped her grenade while adjusting her blouse no one would ever know that we had died for modesty. Finally she borrowed a hairpin from a passenger and locked the grenade handle with it.

We were really crowded, and the terrorists, whose interest it was to reduce tension and free the aisles, sent the passengers they considered harmless—children and their mothers—to the buffer zone in the front of the plane. As a father alone with a child, I was allowed to rejoin my son and thus reaped an unexpected dividend from the solidarity of two liberation movements, the women's and the Palestinians'.

It was a choice observation post. We were ordered to lower the shades of the windows, but I asked the woman in front of me to have her little boy play with the blind. She would lower it, he would raise it, that was the game. I saw outside only intermittently, but at least I saw.

A pious Jew got up, put on his phylacteries and shawl, and said his prayers without anyone trying to stop him. The scene reminded me of a photograph taken in Yad Vachem, in Jerusalem, where a mausoleum, a synagogue, and archives are dedicated to the memory of victims of Nazism. On our last day in the City of David, Guillaume and I had gone where everything ends and everything begins, to the capital of the kingdom of striped ghosts, a museum-necropolis, history's largest cemetery—where not a single corpse rests. Only names are there, the names, all that remains of these dead, the names and the memory. Among the photos I looked at a hundred times, in the vague hope of finding my father's face, there was one of an old Jew at prayer, surrounded by sniggering German privates, one of whom was cutting off the venerable locks with a pair of scissors. I had explained the phylacteries to Guillaume and how they symbolize the link between man and his God, from the arm to the forehead.

"Look, Papa," Guillaume said, "just like the photograph."

But this time no one cut the Jew's locks.

We stopped over in Benghazi, where a Libyan official not without humor came aboard and welcomed us in very guttural English. A woman began to feel faint. With the help of a doctor she succeeded in persuading the terrorists that she was about to have a miscarriage. Thus Patricia Heyman was freed. When she came to get her things she whispered "good luck" to us.

In the seats in the front of the plane, on the lefthand side, there were two large bags in which the terrorists stored their weapons. It was tempting. But the terrorists were always well distributed in the plane, and one couldn't predict what the reaction of the Libyan soldiers would be.

We left Benghazi for an unknown destination. The leader of the terrorists, a blond, chubby German about thirty years old, having gained confidence in the people in the cockpit, began to spend more time with the passengers, trying to smile and even to joke. He went to great lengths to calm his companions, especially the two young Arabs, who were still very nervous. For once, I was rather glad that I was an insomniac. As the plane pushed toward the south and into the night, the terrorists became less tense and some passengers went to sleep. It was the only escape possible. Even Guillaume stopped asking questions and dozed off on my shoulder. I thought about the possible landing places. I was very much afraid of the south of the Arabian Peninsula: South Yemen or worse, the Dofar Province in rebellion. I preferred a well-established sovereign state with a seat in the United Nations and numerous diplomatic ties. So I was relieved when we landed at Entebbe, after circling around with barely four tons of fuel left, just enough for about a half-hour more of flying. As soon as we landed, the woman in front of me had a nervous fit, which was quite genuine to judge by the traces her fingernails left on my hands. Dumbfounded at the sight of Mama stamping both her feet right there, her son fortunately remained quiet.

Before long I was able to make out in the dawn the Africa I was fond of: the savannah, the groves of tall, leafy trees, large El Greco clouds. On this high plateau at least we would not suffer from heat. What irony it was to land in the country that had been offered to the Jews for their State at the turn of the century! If they had not refused, perhaps today we would be in the hands of Ugandan terrorists.

Once everyone was more or less awake, the German read a long manifesto in rather good English. It was a jumble of Ulrike Meinhoff and the Palestinian revolution, of imperialism and French guilt at having provided Israel with arms and an atomic reactor—in short, a leftist stew à la Baader, the kind that is regularly served up in certain Third and Fourth World newspapers, and even from the rostrum of the United Nations. It had to be translated into French. The five or six members of the crew seated nearby were exhausted, and they looked at each other like pupils who have been asked for a volunteer to go to the blackboard. So I went. The German handed me the poorly typed page and the megaphone, and I gave an almost faithful translation.

I took the opportunity to glance into the half-open

bags in front of me: there were a few grenades of a model I had never seen, a few handguns, and a submachine gun loading-clip—not bad for hand luggage! The terrorists were less and less cautious. Sometimes three of them would be in the front of the plane at once, guns in their belts with the hammers lowered, grenades in their pockets; clearly they had won the first round.

Always the humorist, the German took the microphone to thank us for having chosen Air France. He said he hoped we were satisfied with the flight and that he hoped to see us again soon on this airline. The tension had been so great that it had to ease, and there was a general impression—with no basis in logic or fact—that our misadventure had come to an end. Even the captain, speaking first in French and then in his English, told us "the bad dream is finished." For him and his colleagues, who had been in the cockpit for twenty-six hours, this was true to some extent. But in fact, it was merely a change of scene. After the plane had taxied around, we disembarked, with no regrets. As we entered the unused air terminal, the captain said to me: "We must get some sleep, especially if we are going to be flying again soon, so do your best." He was an optimist.

A French plane full of Jews, diverted by a group of terrorists led by two Germans, carrying my elder son and me, so shortly after my trip to Bolivia and the past—it was difficult for me to believe in this hiccup of history, which seemed to have a personal rendezvous in store for me. All the characters were in place for the psychodrama. I found myself thirty-three years back in time. But, in the face of danger, this time the son was with the father.

Settling in was rather orderly. The first to arrive sat on uncomfortable, well-worn red imitation-leather armchairs, the others on the ground. We had to fill out police forms bearing the Palestinian seal. Oh, the symbols of sovereignty! Then we had to get organized.

The crew's exhaustion, in addition to my linguistic abilities and perhaps also the sympathy that a bachelor father inspires, quickly turned me into the interpreter and intermediary between terrorists and hostages. The terrorists from the plane were soon joined by three older comrades, one of whom we nicknamed Groucho Marx because of his cap, his moustache, and his odd gait, or "the Peruvian" because he had lived in Latin America for a long time. Depending on the person he was speaking to, he claimed to be Colombian, Chilean, or Peruvian, a true member of the Fifth International. In any case, he knew Ciudad Nueva well. My Spanish became useful; it is a warm language which encourages familiarity. In French it can take twenty years to reach the familiar "tu" stage, and by then it is often too late. In Spanish, ten minutes are enough for people of comparable age and status. Even though the first evening, when we had spoken English—a language he did not know well and which seemed to displease him, perhaps as the language of "imperialists"— he had put his Kalachnikov against my stomach to stop me from turning off too many lights—we were soon saying "tu" and "ti."

Our selves were stripped bare, and each of us reacted in accordance with his deepest nature. Some thought of themselves first, like the woman who grabbed two cartons of the cigarettes distributed by the crew. When, at the insistence of several passengers, I asked her to give them up, she said by way of excuse: "I don't smoke, you know. They are for my son" (who was not there). This was undoubtedly her way of telling herself that she would see him again. Many stuffed themselves with rice and bananas even though food—rather mediocre at that—was always ample and on time. It is true that eating is a way of relieving anxiety, of alleviating fear which gnaws at the plexus. To eat is to live. I said to a Moroccan Jewish woman whose legs spread from the pressure of the fat around her thighs whenever she sat down: "Why don't you take advantage of the opportunity to diet?"

Her reply was a weak, humiliated smile. I was ashamed of my cruel and useless remark.

A well-meaning Frenchwoman, obviously more knowledgeable about diet than geography, said to me: "Ask them for some apples. That would be enough. And it's healthier."

"But madam, we are around the equator."

She gave me a pained look of incomprehension.

More serious was the problem of the pious Jews, who refused to touch non-kosher food. A quick census turned up twenty, and we decided that they would be served first, before the rice was sprinkled with the liquid that was supposed to give it taste. The next morning, sixty people claimed to be religious observants—and were therefore served first.

But those who thought of others before themselves came out much better than the selfish. We developed stalag reflexes: to set up a library, organize meals, give lectures. The flight engineer gave a talk in French on our plane, the Airbus, then a novelty, and an Israeli passenger who had been posted in Uganda during the honeymoon between Israel and Black Africa gave one on Uganda. Recent political developments were not part of the curriculum. A Frenchman who was quickly nicknamed "Teach" salvaged fruit-juice cans to make ashtrays for those who were trying to puff away their fears. As for the children, they found it amusing because all parental rules had been shattered. They no longer had to wash, to put on pajamas, or to go to bed early, before the others.

Curiously enough, I felt in my element. I had the impression of finally living out a play that I had rehearsed a thousand times but never performed. Surrounded by Frenchmen and Jews, under the eyes of my son, facing a death that I hardly thought about and to which I was rather indifferent, I felt the important thing was to conduct myself well. I thought a great deal about Laurent, the son who was not with me but was within me. He was so gentle and so intense at the same time, still a child and already a man. I wanted to give him no reason to be ashamed of his father.

How easy it is to die when one doesn't like oneself. How

suspect is heroism, then, how many suicides are disguised as acts of bravery.

The first night in the terminal building, an old Jewish woman, probably of Germanic origin, had a fit of madness. Sitting straight up on her mattress, she began asking louder and louder: "Where am I? Where am I?" Then, suddenly, her voice rose several octaves and she screamed for help, waking some of the children. Several of her neighbors tried to calm her but without success. A few of the children began to cry. Then a member of the crew, the German, and one or two other men took her out of the building, hoping the fresh air would calm her and that, at least, she would not wake up the rest of the children. The old woman rambled incoherently, no doubt believing herself back in the damned days. She took all her money from her blouse and gave it to the crew member, who, not knowing what to do with it, handed it over to the German. Money, the poor security of the hunted; money for the smuggler of refugees, money for the ticket, money for the SS. The money that Jews are reproached and hounded for. At the moment it was useless. Finally the old woman remained alone with her jailor, who shared the same maternal language. He put his arm around her shoulders and tried to quiet her. It was an incredible sight: the young heir of the Nazis speaking in a gentle voice for a good two hours to this old Jewish woman, shaking with spasms. I was sitting on a blanket taken from the plane which Guillaume and I shared for sleeping. He too was awake, of course. Without a word, we looked at the scene illuminated by moonlight, made even brighter by the reflection on nearby Lake Victoria. The old woman began to sob in the German's arms. It was over. I whistled "Mein Yiddische Mama" between my teeth. It pained me to see her abandon herself that way in the arms of a lie.

I had formed a curious relationship with the cherub-faced German who was in charge of the military aspects of the operation. Calm and smiling when there was no reason to be threatening, he reminded me more of Régis Debray, intellectual turned revolutionary, than of Otto Skorzeny, the daredevil SS who spirited Mussolini out of the Abruzzi. Fugitive from the bourgeoisie, an idealist without an ideal to latch onto, he searched in far corners of the world for the exaltation the materialistic West lacked for him. He often tried to justify his unjustifiable presence. "The Palestinian revolution is an integral part of the worldwide revolutionary movement against imperialism in Germany, the United States, Japan, Eritrea." To rationalize having picked on a French plane, he blamed France for all of Israel's sins: the colonization of the Red Sea port of Djibouti "to protect Israeli trade to the port of Eilat," the mandate over Syria and Lebanon, the Algerian war, the Suez expedition, Israel's atomic reactor at Dimona, the Mirages, the unpunished assassinations in the streets of Paris—and that's not all. "Besides, it's useless to try anything with El-Al; they have orders to shoot it out and they have special bullets that won't pierce the fuselage."

He wanted to be called Basil, the given name of Al Khubaisi, a PLO representative assassinated in Paris. I called him Klaus and sometimes Obersturmführer. This postwar child was vulnerable to ideological discussions and I took sadistic delight in baiting him.

"If this lasts a few more nights," I said to him, "one of these old people will die, and even if it is only ten minutes before the time that he or she would have died somewhere else, the whole world will consider you a murderer of the elderly. Furthermore, these people present us with insoluble problems: the man with the heart condition doesn't have his pills, the person with varicose veins can hardly walk, the man with malaria who hasn't had an attack in twenty years was delirious all night. It is in your interest and ours to rid ourselves of them. That was the logic of the SS on the Auschwitz train platform. If you don't want to resemble them you had better free the weak quickly."

Or: "Doesn't it bother you, a leftist revolutionary from a country that made a name for itself by inventing the worst type of fascism, to torment the same victims of this fascism again?"

"No, because my goals are different."

"And the means?"

"Up to now you haven't suffered too much. We have been 'korrect' with you."

Unknowingly, he had revived that forty-year-old adjective.

"True, but we could all have been burnt alive. And besides, you're not keeping us here to educate us."

Or: "Doesn't it bother you, an anticolonialist, to have Arabs as subordinates?"

"No, because I have nothing to gain from it."

"And what about glory?"

How well I understood this German. He was so full of ideas and so empty of love. I had been his brother, his older brother. I manipulated him because he was my enemy but I could just as well have helped him.

Wilfried Boese, if that was his name, was the only terrorist who really had an opportunity to kill hostages when the Israelis attacked. After a moment of hesitation, he turned his weapon away from the hostages, told them to take cover, hurled his grenade uselessly outside, and was killed instantly. No one will ever know the reason for this final switch: was it a moral or a utilitarian reflex? It is difficult to link causes and effects, and the temptation to overestimate one's own role is so great.

In any case, these conversations enabled me to establish a pseudo-egalitarian relationship with him that had its uses. When he showed annoyance with one more problem posed by the elderly passengers: "You don't have to worry about that, Klaus; you are in a job without a future." When the German woman insisted on escorting male Israeli prisoners to the toilet with a gun to their backs: "Does she also hold it for them?" I made a suggestion that seemed to intrigue him: "When you begin to kill the hostages, how will the rest of the world know that they are dead? Because you say so. Then what prevents you from saying so without doing it? Perhaps that way you could combine the advantages of violence and leniency." I didn't much believe what I was saying, but there was no harm in trying. What nonsense was uttered that week! And since then . . .

I devoted myself especially to making material life less uncomfortable, and he helped me. Boese refused only two of the reasonable requests that I made in writing on behalf of the hostages. I was thankful for my habit of always carrying what I needed for work and for the night in hand luggage, because we didn't have access to our baggage in the hold.

We obtained mattresses rather quickly, thanks to the Canadian Aid Agency, whose stamp was still on them, and also some towels. Since there were not enough for everyone, I asked, through the plane's megaphone, that those who shared everything in life share towels as well. Finally, I succeeded in arranging for the sale in the terminal of duty-free products from the airport. The two young Ugandan vendors were struggling so hard with the arithmetic of currency conversion that I came to the rescue. Armed with my pocket calculator, I presided over the only session of Entebbe's ephemeral foreign-currency market. Only spot transactions, no futures. In spite of the insistence of one of the female passengers, the Israeli pound was not quoted.

In order to prevent the first customers from buying out everything they had, I asked our sellers how often they intended to call on us. Many of the hostages managed to laugh when I announced that we would be entitled to a weekly visit.

These little comforts made the waiting and relationships tolerable. In uniform again, the captain began to get a grip on himself. He tried to restore the morale of the passengers, male and female. Conversing with two Jewish-American women academics—the type who would spend hours comparing the use of the subjunctive imperfect in Plautus and Pliny the Younger—he turned to me: "How does one say '*sieste crapuleuse*' in English?"

"Try '*matinée.*'" Gallic humor did not lose its prerogatives, even if he had mistaken his public.

I carefully avoided Brigitte Kuhlmann, who practiced terrorism as psychotherapy. Lacking the affection of adults, this former student of pedagogy sought that of children. I sent Guillaume to divert her when I wanted to be sure that she would not meddle in a conversation. I opposed her only once. It was the first night, when ten mattresses had to be shared among over two hundred and fifty persons. She wanted them for the children. A number of them were already asleep curled up against their mothers, while many old people were having difficulty finding a restful position on the seats or on the floor. Even she eventually bowed to the obvious.

People in need of a father came to me with the strangest problems: a woman in her fifties was robbed of her only pair of panties, which she had washed and hung out to dry; another passenger did not know what to do with the fish she was bringing back to Paris—it was beginning to smell; some Greeks wanted me to demand that they be freed since they had absolutely nothing to do with the issue at hand; an Israeli informed me that he was not Jewish and told me his wishes regarding funeral arrangements; a Colombian woman from Medellín, still a flirt though no longer in her prime, had noticed that our captors were talking about freeing the elderly and confided that she was not as young as she looked; a diamond dealer told me, in the German's presence, that the delay was costing him money.

I was acceptable as a spokesman to most of the groups there: to the Jews because I was Jewish, to the French because I was French, to the English and Spanish speakers because I knew their languages, and to the terrorists because I was a Jew after their own hearts: neither Israeli nor pious, and with influence over the hostages. As for the Israelis, they differed: a woman has told me since that she was sure I was a terrorist planted among the hostages— how else would I have been able to establish such an effective relationship with our captors? Another woman thought I was an Israeli pilot who had succeeded in hiding his identity! She spoke to me in Hebrew several times to see if I would react. I didn't, and for good reason.

On the second day, I had to translate the terrorists' ultimatum. They demanded freedom for fifty-three prisoners being held mostly in Israel, but also in Switzerland, Germany, and Kenya. Only two names were familiar to me: Okamoto, the sole survivor of the Lod massacre, and Capucci, the priest–weapons smuggler. The ultimatum would expire at noon on Thursday, two days later.

That same day Idi Amin paid us a visit with semi-muted fanfare. He wore a freshly pressed paratrooper uniform, cap, and shoes with Gucci-type buckles. I felt deeply humiliated by the spontaneous applause that greeted his arrival and departure. An Israeli even felt the need to shake his hand effusively. I went around the room in an attempt to convince people that we had nothing to gain from lowering ourselves in that way. On Amin's second visit, after his henchmen had retrieved the ten-gallon Borsalino blown off his stately head by the impertinent puff of wind created by His Bigness's helicopter, the applause was hardly less prolonged. A little frustrated, I nevertheless translated the words of the boxer-turned-king, making corrections where I thought it was useful to do so—for example, when he claimed to be president of Africa instead of outgoing president of the Organization of African Unity. Above all, I toned down the menacing character of certain words: "If your governments care about your lives. . . ." His English was acceptable, his delivery slow, perhaps because of the syphilis for which the Israelis had treated him in the past. His remarks were simpleminded: "I have visited the Jews in their church in Syria, they were very happy. The Jews of Syria live with the Arabs and that's what the Palestinians want, not war."

Our voices—his and mine—were sometimes made inaudible by the roar of a low-flying Mig passing back and forth, probably to discourage any attempt at revolt, or perhaps to help us take down the clothes we had washed and hung up to dry.

The separation from the Israelis, on Tuesday evening the twenty-ninth, was the first great ground test. But it didn't happen the way it was described in numerous sensation-seeking articles, books, and films. "The Peruvian" came over and told us that the persons whose names were going to be read out were to go to the next room, which had just been prepared. By the third mangled name, it was evident, even to those with only a smattering of biblical knowledge, that the names, especially the given names, were Hebrew: Eytan, Ilan, Noam, Hannah, Akiva, Uzi. No one moved. I asked the German if freedom of movement would be maintained between the two groups, who had to use the same toilets. His promise that it would be was mostly broken.

The captain took the loudspeaker: "It is we who have asked our guards for more space. All they did was to grant our request, so there is no cause for alarm." Did he understand that it was not more space but the criterion of separation that was the problem? That very evening, I suggested to him and the flight engineer that there was no reason for the crew to endorse the terrorists' distinctions and that two or three of the twelve members of the crew might ask to be assigned to the room with the Israeli passengers. Both of them asked for time to think about it and to consult with other members of the crew. The next morning the flight engineer came to me with a reply that won my respect for its candor: "We have wives and children. If there is any shooting it will be in there first. We are not heroes, we prefer to remain here."

I had to remind the captain of my question. He, too, said no, but how different were the grounds for his refusal: "It's not worth the trouble. We'll visit them often. It's no use complicating things." As a matter of fact, the captain, other members of the crew, and a few passengers did pay frequent visits to the "people of the ghetto" separated from the others by a wooden crossbar—and much more.

Among the non-Israelis, there were a few doubtful cases that gave rise to questioning. On this occasion, one of us became so entangled in his answers that it cost him two broken ribs. I asked the little group that was worried about him: "Does anyone really know his nationality?" The captain replied: "He has a French passport, but physically he is very marked."

I was crushed by that reply. It gave substance once again to a racial definition of nationality, thirty years after Vichy! The hostage in question would not have caused even a novice physiognomist to hesitate. But the sole objective of the members of this ephemeral and infamous profession of the Vichy era was to identify by facial features who was Jewish, not who was French. Besides, the man, like many Sephardim, was no less an Arab in "type."

Were the two sides of France with us even there—the light and the dark, the France of Collenot and the France of Ramass, the France of Zola and the France of Maurras, the France of Brassens and the France of Brasillach, the

France of 1793 and of 1940, the France of Jean Jaurès and of Pierre Poujade, the France of Beuve-Méry and the France of *Minute*, the France of the Council of State* and the France of the reason of State, the France of the Prefect of Police and the France of the Prefect of Chartres, the France that I loved so much that I could die for her and the France that despised me to death, the France for which I had only to be and the France for which I could never do enough, the one that sent me to La Paz? But this was no time for historical reflection. Perhaps I saw only what I feared. Perhaps the captain was not really such a bad fellow, merely unaware that he had just poured salt into a still-open wound.

Then came my own private test: separation from my son.

Guillaume was part of the contingent of forty-seven persons—children, mothers, old people, plus a clever little Moroccan and his family—who were freed on Wednesday. The criteria for this first release were rather simple: the children, their mothers, most of the old peo-

---

*The writer Zola forced the reopening of the Dreyfus case by publishing an open letter to the President of the Republic, *J'Accuse*; Maurras was the founder and guiding spirit of the Action Française. The late Brassens was an iconoclastic, somewhat anarchist poet and singer; Brasillach, a talented collaborationist writer executed at the Liberation. Jaurès was a pacifist Socialist leader assassinated just before the outbreak of World War I; Poujade, an ephemeral leader of a right-wing shopkeepers' movement. Beuve-Méry was a member of the French Resistance and founder of the highly respected *Le Monde*; *Minute*, a right-wing tabloid. The Council of State is the French equivalent of the United States Supreme Court, dealing exclusively with matters to which the State is a party. The Council of State has generally been the defender of individual rights.

ple and the sick, provided that they were neither Israelis nor nationals of certain Arab countries that forbid their citizens to travel to Israel. The evening before, the terrorists had gone around the room hastily making up their list. Guillaume had grabbed one of them by the sleeve: "Put my father on the list, put my father on the list," he repeated in his broken English. "Guillaume, one doesn't beg these people." I raised my voice to him for the first time during our detention. But I was touched.

The cuffs of his jeans, which his mother had bought to last him until he was at least eighteen, were filled with harmless personal messages and the professional memorandum I had written on the plane. My only request was that an account I had written of my Bolivian adventure be published in the event of my death. Guillaume came over, hugged me, and said in an almost steady voice: "Papa, you remember how much you missed your own father? So please don't play cowboy." One of the hostages, who has since written a book about our adventure, which at least has the merit of being a firsthand account, described the scene as follows: "The young thirteen-year-old boy is called. He hesitates to leave his father. The father—and who wouldn't understand—has difficulty controlling his emotions. He pushes the son toward the door. The young boy leaves, head and shoulders straight, without luggage. The self-control that he exercises with all his strength is, it seems to me, a deliberate manifestation of the affection he wants to express to his father. I myself have a thirteen-year-old son waiting for me in France. . . . I find myself hoping that he would display such an admirable attitude in similar circumstances."*

There is no doubt that Guillaume was of considerable help to me during this adventure. He was my backbone, my mirror. He witnessed every act, every word. I was proud of him. I was proud of him for organizing a football game when I got permission for the children to play on the tarmac in a rectangle formed by the twenty or so Ugandan soldiers who helped the terrorists guard us. There were only seven of them, and they too had to sleep.

My son's departure left me alone and free.

With the most vulnerable gone, the rest of us began to organize ourselves for a stay which I imagined would be long. We had no news from the outside—the German had rejected my request for newspapers—and tongues were wagging away. Our "yachtsman"—an Englishman returning from a cruise and dressed appropriately—devised a clever system of placing the chairs in a square with a daytime position and a nighttime position, if you please, which made it possible to move around during the day without bumping into what served as our beds. "Barracks" were formed along lines of linguistic and other affinities. I had a choice and opted for a French group, which included a couple of Air France employees returning from vacation.

"So much for 'service-plus'!"

*Claude Moufflet, *Otages à Kampala* (Paris: Presses de la Cité, 1976), p. 101.

Using the criteria of the first release of hostages, the engineer and I drew up a list of sick or elderly people who, through weakness, ignorance, or timidity, had not made themselves known the first time: an Englishman with a heart ailment who had not noticed anything, an old woman who had been in the toilet at the time, and others who simply exceeded the number the terrorists were willing to release.

Nevertheless, the second release was very different from the first. On learning that Israel had accepted the principle of negotiation, the terrorists postponed the date of the ultimatum until Sunday noon and decided to free another contingent of non-Israelis. We were asked to draw up very quickly a list of all those in the non-Israeli room. When I came to the crew, grouped near the bar where no one had drunk anything for years, the Peruvian yelled at me: "Not the crew!"* Then the terrorists ticked off the names of those who could be freed, with a few cross-outs and write-overs. They wanted to proceed as quickly as possible in order to prevent us from exchanging messages and to reduce the duration of what promised to be a tense period. And they were also very much afraid of crowd movements. One of the Arabs began to read the list of those who could leave. But the names were so varied and so complicated that he stumbled over each syllable, and even some of those whose names were called failed to react. I took the list from him and began calling out the names that were familiar to

*Moufflet, *Otages à Kampala*, p. 123.

me. The entire Diaspora was there, or almost—from Europe, North and South America, North Africa; only Russian Jews were missing. In addition, there were the season's tourists, a few merchants, and a few lost souls who had boarded the plane in Athens: a Korean, an important blue-eyed Jordanian, three Greek sailors, the yachtsman. I fell silent, stunned, when, after having read an elderly couple's name, I noticed that their son, who was in the prime of life, was not among those scheduled to leave. The parents were already on their feet, expecting their son's name to be called out next. The flight engineer, who had observed that I was stymied, whispered to me: "Tell him that the father can't walk without his son." I used this little argument and the terrorist let himself be convinced.

The criteria for this second release of hostages were somewhat confused: a hundred people or so were to be freed, provided that they were neither members of the crew nor Israelis, real or suspected. Some hostages whose names and behavior made it obvious that they were Jews were also freed, most notably two very pious Brazilians with yarmulkes, who had originally been placed in the room with the Israelis by the German woman but who had been transferred by the Peruvian.

Once the operation was completed, three groups remained: the Israelis in their room, the crew by the bar, and about thirty leftovers grouped in a corner near the bay windows.

The few foreigners in the Israeli room were persons who had more or less long-term visas and two pious Jewish couples, one Belgian, the other American. Film-makers and other producers of recent history were able to use these facts, if they knew them, to make the chord of Auschwitz vibrate by implying that the terrorists had separated the Jews from the others. An error involving four persons, one of whom had fumbled his way into being disliked by everyone, does not change the distinction the terrorists tried to enforce: separate the real or potential Israelis from the others. There were also errors in the other direction, of which much less has been said, and for good reason: a high-ranking officer of the Israeli army was among the second group of hostages to be released. Many Jews wearing a yarmulke or a large Star of David were freed that day. As I have said, we got the Ugandans, to whom kosher cuisine was a mystery, not to put sauce on the rice so that the pious Jews, Israelis or not, could eat according to Jewish dietary laws.

No, Entebbe was not Auschwitz, in spite of what the sensation-hungry journalists and film-makers said. It was not Auschwitz, even if we were tempted to take our fears for realities. At Entebbe, Brigitte Kuhlmann was not Ilse Koch (the "Witch of Buchenwald," famous for her collection of lampshades made of human skin, preferably tattooed), even if they belonged to the same family of psychopaths. At Entebbe, the terrorists had a concrete goal—the freeing of fifty-three prisoners—which one can disapprove of but which is not a utopian, arrogant, and insane redefinition of man. Entebbe was the Ritz compared to Auschwitz. Even if hostages had been killed off—and it was easy to see who would be the first among them—it would not have been an Auschwitz; it is important how and why one dies! The terrorists would have killed the hostages as they had taken them, efficiently but without cruelty. They would have killed Israeli hostages not because of their Jewishness but because Israel occupied—wrongfully in the terrorists' eyes—land that they considered theirs. The two Germans were only tools who had come in search of an illusory solution to problems they carried within themselves.

It has been said, written, allowed to be said, and allowed to be written that the crew "refused to be repatriated with the Jewish hostages."* If the members of the crew had had a chance to leave, it is quite likely that they would have refused. They had talked it over and, in spite of some resistance, had prepared the reply one might expect. Besides, it would have been pointless for all twelve of them to remain voluntarily. Honor would have been just as intact if two or three of the highest-ranking crew members had stayed. The plenipotentiary minister sent by France had tried unsuccessfully to obtain the release of the stewardesses. But the question of the crew's release was never raised and could not be raised, at least for those who were needed to operate the Airbus. Amin might ask the terrorists to leave; he could be overthrown, assassinated. The terrorists, who were not stupid, had no reason to deprive themselves of their means of transportation. The crew was

*Tony Williamson, *Entebbe*, Plon; caption of photo preceding p. 97.

not invited to leave, and so they remained with almost all the Israelis, as did several others, French or not, Jewish or not. They were very sad that noon, the youngest of the stewardesses letting fresh tears run down her cheeks. They were hostages like the others, some close to the political drama that had brought them there, others very remote from it.

The third group was ill-defined: young people, single people, suspects in the eyes of the terrorists. They were the remainders of a long division that did not come out even. I noticed a young Canadian woman crying silently. I pointed out to one of the terrorists that her name had been ticked off as someone to be released and then crossed out in an ambiguous way. After a quick glance at the paper and a few simple questions, he motioned to her to leave. It was then that I realized there was still room for maneuver. I applied myself to getting a few more people out. The captain and the flight engineer did the same. It was incredible that I, a son of Auschwitz, could walk around, list in hand, holding a small particle of the odious divine power, among hostages, most of them Jewish. Secretary of the arbitrary, I could have some influence on how to divide the souls, who might live and who might not. I had to find arguments acceptable to the terrorists.

The first one that came to mind concerned the passengers who had boarded the plane in Athens. Thus I was able to obtain the release of two American couples, one named Rabinowitz. I was prepared to insist that theirs was a Russian name, but the question never came up; the plane ticket was enough. An American doctor had confided that he had a heart ailment and told me of his wishes should an accident occur. I described his case as a little worse than it was, pushed it, and they let him leave. Another doctor, this one a Frenchman, showed his visiting card to prove his residence. But the name "France" did not appear on the card, and the doctor lived in a suburb unknown to the terrorist. We succeeded in convincing him that it was near Paris.

This terrorist was rather understanding. He, too, wanted to be loved, by the whole world and by me; he even showed himself capable of closing his eyes to a maneuver of mine an inept passenger had brought to light. One cannot overestimate the importance in such circumstances of establishing cordial relations beyond ideological differences. But where does cordiality stop and complicity begin? Should I regret having offered a little cigar to one of the two young Arab terrorists? He was asking my advice about improving his English.

I could no longer find any arguments to use for those who were left. One of them began to beg in Arabic, almost on his knees, arousing the anger of one of the terrorists. Servility was as useless and dangerous as arrogance.

It was over. I took the loudspeaker one last time to ask the freed hostages to leave behind the articles they had bought that very morning. Then I sat down, exhausted. I felt drained. The terrorists who were standing around also sat down. One of them joked: "You have been so useful that you have to stay." My name was indeed on the list of those to be released but I had not read it aloud. When the flight engineer asked me if I was leaving, I had given him a noncommittal answer. I was wondering just what to do.

All that would be waiting for me when I returned would be loneliness and the agony of divorce proceedings. Here I had a role, at least some small usefulness. The personal risk was not very great. It seemed out of the question that I, or the crew, would be among the hostages to be shot. To stay, that would be to affirm my identity, my solidarity, my courage; to stay would be to find in Entebbe what I had gone to seek in Bolivia. The glory I had hoped for so much, that I had lain in wait for, was coming to me here, and in the form I had dreamt of: Franco-Jewish. History was lending me a convenient hand; French and Israelis, Jews and non-Jews, couldn't help admiring me. To stay would be to belong, certainly at the bottom of the list, but still, in the company of those who had chosen to join the deportees in their Calvary—Korczak, Pilecki* . . . to stay would be to reserve for myself a stool by the Righteous. Yes, but to stay would serve no purpose except for myself, for my glory—and I knew enough about the thirst for glory to resist it. To give my place to an Israeli woman and her children? I had considered that; a nun released with the first group had tried it without success. We were not fungible in the eyes of the terrorists.

*Janos Korczak was a Polish child psychologist and head of an orphanage who insisted on accompanying his Jewish wards to the camps and was murdered there. Witold Pilecki engineered his own deportation to Auschwitz, where he organized and led an underground resistance movement.

What could I do if I left? One idea had occurred to me. I didn't dare put much faith in it; nevertheless, it assailed me again. Djibouti, the last French territory in Africa within easy reach, the distance from Paris to Madrid. Djibouti, where reinforcements of the Foreign Legion had been sent to quash the troubles related to the territory's imminent independence. Djibouti, where, with little damage, an elite unit had freed children held hostage on a bus. The Israelis couldn't intervene, they were too far away. Besides, the hijacking had occurred on a French aircraft—that is, on French territory. The passengers were a French responsibility. Was it possible that France would not consider using her armed forces to counter such an affront? That did not require questioning her oily sympathies. Who could hold it against her? Surely not the Arab countries. Most of them had sincerely condemned all hijackings and must have been concerned to see France so poorly rewarded for the understanding she had shown them. The African governments? Perhaps they would protest as a matter of form, but in their heart of hearts, they probably hoped that this would cost his throne to the bloody clown who had done so much harm to their cause. Uganda? What did France have in Uganda more precious than the hundred or so men, women, and children placed under the protection of her flag?

Of course that was the solution, and someone was needed to provide the necessary details: how many terrorists, with what weapons and at which guard posts; where best to enter to minimize the risk that stray bullets would hit the hostages. Someone who would be able to prove that, contrary to what we had been told, the cases stored in the Israeli room did not contain explosives. What were the functions, positions, equipment of the Ugandan soldiers? Where did those not on guard duty sleep? Perhaps some of the freed hostages had observed these details, but how could one be sure? How could one know whether the French authorities would be able to locate and question them? I was a reserve officer; I knew which people to see; I would be able to prove that the terrorists and their Ugandan accomplices, with their minds at rest because of the distance, did not present a very formidable obstacle.

I got up, retrieved my pen from the terrorist who had borrowed it, went to say goodbye to the crew, promised to call this one or that one, and paid a last visit to the Israelis. Emma, the woman my son had sat next to on the plane, saw my eyes glistening:

"Why are you crying?"

"Because it brings back memories."

For a moment, I hesitated to leave my toilet kit, the contents of which I had so meticulously arranged. I had considered staying, and now I was reluctant to leave some razor behind.

I took down my clothing that was drying in front of the building which had sheltered us for nearly a week and got into the bus.

Some passengers regained their tourist reflexes in the new terminal while waiting for the plane. Even the rice-in-sauce that was still served to us tasted better.

Before allowing us to board our plane out, the Ugandan authorities indulged themselves in the ridiculous exercise of submitting us to a careful search, in case one of us had concealed a weapon with which to hijack the special return plane. At takeoff, our eyes turned to the portholes on the left, through which we could see the terminal that still held over a hundred hostages. The anxiety of perhaps having made the wrong choice gripped me.

Air France offered us champagne. A woman passenger, filled with gratitude, didn't know how to thank me. "Without you my husband wouldn't be here." I thought that I had behaved decently, and I was applauded when I returned from the cabin, where I had been invited by the captain while we were flying over Libya, lit up by flares.

The yachtsman, so British, stopped me as I was going back to my seat:

"One of the things that surprised me during this adventure is that you seemed prepared for it."

Actually, I *was* prepared for it, by thirty years of fantasies, reading, and dreams. I had been given the opportunity to live through a version, though certainly very watered down, of my nightmare. Had I lived it well? Could I wake up at last?

PART IV

In Coventry

Most of the graves are surmounted by a Roman cross, but one also sees a few six-pointed stars and inscriptions in Hebrew characters. . . . That is what [the Resistance at] Les Glières was: an unqualified brotherhood. . . .

—Description of Morette Cemetery by François Musard in *Les Glières*

CHAPTER 10 *Awakening at Noon*

It was a pleasant surprise to find my future ex-wife waiting for me in the VIP lounge at Orly. We embraced each other almost as warmly as a real couple, but we were interrupted by an official of the Ministry of the Interior, whose sober countenance and attire vouched for his importance. He wanted to see me alone, and urgently. I was filled with joy. France needed me. I gave the official a knowing smile. We arranged to meet a few hours later.

At the time agreed upon, the appointment was neither kept nor canceled. I did receive visitors, but they were not French.

Then the Israelis landed at Entebbe and freed the remaining hostages.

Three days later, on the following Tuesday, a young French official came by to take my deposition. With a long face, I repeated what I had told the newspapers. He returned on Friday to have me sign the five copies that he himself had typed, with carbons. It was a translation into dreary government jargon of what the newspapers were full of, which no longer mattered.

I corrected a few spelling errors; he begged me to excuse his typing: "We don't have the means of the private sector, you know." Perhaps in an attempt to win forgiveness for these mistakes, he showed me how to dismantle the large-calibre weapon he was carrying and, with many understatements flattering to me, spoke of the other testimonies that he had laboriously collected for the sole benefit of the archives.

Even though France had not come to the rescue of the passengers in her charge, I thought it would at least be possible to rejoice together over the success of the Israeli operation. The Air France employee with whom I had shared quarters at Entebbe asked me, as spokesman for the hostages, to write a letter to his management praising the crew's behavior. In the elation of the liberation, I threw my reservations to the wind. There should be no false notes in the general rejoicing. So I wrote a fine letter which omitted the malodorous details, suggesting unity of behavior among the crew, which had numbered twelve very different people. Without writing anything false, thanks to the marvelous instrument that is the French language, I succeeded in bending the truth. I, too, wanted things to be as I would have wished them.

But official France, annoyed that Israel had succeeded in her stead, and without even consulting her, maintained a pinched silence. She offered neither congratulations nor thanks. The secretary-general of the Elysée, one of the first in France to be informed, did present his felicitations on the telephone "in a personal capacity"; the prefecture of police was unusually nice to those who needed new documents; Air France was unusually generous in compensating the hostages for lost baggage; but silence, a great milky silence, prevailed. I wanted to cry out, but I no longer had a loudspeaker.

Even the French diplomat who had visited the unfortunate Dora Bloch* in Mulago Hospital a few hours before she was murdered was forbidden to tell her sons anything: it was necessary not to contradict Amin, who claimed that she had been freed along with the other hostages. To ensure his silence, this specialist in Africa was transferred from Uganda to Central America. Machiavelli, how many exercises in unnecessary humiliation have been committed in thy name!

"We could have done the same as the Israelis," the Minister of Defense let slip. Did he mean *could* or *should*? And didn't "could" make "should" more imperative? No, these hostages were not worth the bones of a Pomeranian legionnaire, as Bismarck might have said. Kolwezi† yes, Entebbe no. To make the world forget her failure to act,

---

*An Israeli-British woman in her seventies who had to be hospitalized during her sojourn in Entebbe. After she recovered, the Italian doctor responsible had kept her at the hospital, thinking that she would be better off there than at the airport. Consequently she was the only hostage not to be brought back by the Israelis. The night after the raid, she was wrested from her bed and murdered by Amin's police. Her remains were recovered after the fall of the Ugandan dictator and buried in Jerusalem on June 5, 1979.

†A town in Shaba, the mineral-rich province of Zaïre, where French legionnaires, in 1978, were dispatched to rescue a group of Europeans besieged by black irregulars.

France needed some heroes, heroes who would be hers, heroes who would be her. France is the State, and what could be closer to the State than the uniformed servants of its own nationalized airline?

The captain was hastily made a chevalier of the Legion of Honor and summoned to the Elysée to grace the table of the king of Spain, who had come to visit his brother beyond the mountains. The rest of the crew was awarded the Cross of Merit and even an obscure medal of French courtesy. The press, books, films—including the Israeli film—joined in the chorus: the crew was composed solely of lion-hearted heroes who had protected their terrified passengers. In spite of a few individual reservations, the crew allowed themselves to be used, for even thus they continued to serve. For once, the goat was beribboned instead of being chased into the desert.

In the aristocratic republic that is France, only those who serve the State are noble. The elitist prejudice, a distant cousin of racism, worked instinctively without anyone's even thinking of protesting. The entire crew, and only the crew, became heroes. There were other French hostages who had remained with the Israelis until the end, but only the crew was worthy of praise because collectively they symbolized France.

But no one should cast the smallest shadow on their new-minted glory. Only former passenger-hostages who could not express themselves easily in French were invited to appear on radio and television, leaving the screen free for those in whose interest it was to save the State's face.

Certain details were expanded while others disappeared. Roles were glossed over. Thus the truth was gradually retouched. I received a brief letter of thanks from the director-general of Air France, then there was silence. I had existed for five days, and suddenly I was erased. No one needed a spoilsport.

Was I jealous of these cut-rate decorations fallen from the sky? Jealous of the country's expression of esteem and affection, of the increased vitality and virility that come from righteous pride? Sincerely, I do not think so. None of the hostages had voluntarily risked life or even an hour's freedom; none deserved a Cross. But I had a tremendous feeling of injustice, of exclusion. Again I was rejected by France.

Almost without hesitation, I had refused useless glory, and I was now in the position of having to justify myself: "How is it," I was asked, "that a gentile crew stayed with the Jews voluntarily while you left?" And again, "You're lucky that you were calling yourself Cojot." And again and again and again.

Could it be that the symbol is more precious than the truth, fantasy more important than effectiveness? I began to doubt. I punished myself for having permitted my father to leave for the East alone, why shouldn't others wound me with their words for having abandoned the hostages at Entebbe? O, the absurdity of "togetherness," which had cost the lives of so many families that had chosen the illusory warmth of a nest over the spreading of risk, the security of dispersion! Anne Frank's family became famous through her, but the Joffo sons are alive.* One doesn't put all one's children in a single basket.

Had I stayed at Entebbe, I would have been scarcely more useful to the remaining hostages than I would have been to my father in Lyon. I would not have been able to prevent them from being murdered. But isn't the greatest solidarity in death, even in futile death? Had I not been strengthened by my son's presence? And what if there had been no Israeli operation, or if it had failed? No doubt my body would have remained alive, but what new tortures would my soul have invented for the two of us?

After Entebbe—eight months after—I resigned myself to joining in a lawsuit against Air France. It would have taken so little for me to withdraw. But no, all they left me with was money, filthy money, that poor consolation of the unloved.

After Entebbe, our captain recognized one evening among his passengers about to leave for Madrid the only terrorist who had escaped death—at the time of the raid he was dining at Amin's—the one who had closed his eyes to my subterfuge at the time of the second release of hostages. Alerted, the police at Orly referred the problem up. After half an hour the reply came: there was no valid reason to delay the bearer of a Syrian passport even though an eye-witness had formally identified him as a person who had

*Joseph Joffo, now a Parisian barber-writer, and his brother, not yet in their teens during the war, were sent away by their father and thus escaped the Nazis. He describes their experiences in *Un sac de billes*.

held the passengers of a French aircraft hostage and caused four of them to die. And once again he was coming from Entebbe! Our captain, sole master on board after God and the ministry, was the one who had to escort this passenger to impunity.

If the terrorist had been tried, I would have testified in his favor. But it was not up to a bureaucrat to decide to let him go, while alerting the Spaniards to ease his conscience. As for the captain, perhaps he could have used his authority to take this worrisome passenger off the plane; the Civil Aviation Code formally spells out his right to do so. At Barajas Airport the terrorist was obliged to strip and submit to a body search. That was the extent of his punishment.

After Entebbe, my apparent geographical instability finally took on meaning for me. What up to then had seemed to be a shapeless itinerary suddenly took form, my Allied-Van-itis could be diagnosed, my mothlike moves became clearer. I was never more French than when I was abroad, where my characteristics, my accent, stood out. How happy I was during my first trip out of the country to be recognized everywhere as French, even though that was hardly flattering in the eyes of the natives, who were tired of being invaded every summer by Pierre, Paul, and Jacques, the conquerors of little English girls.

But soon distance weighed, and I returned to the land of my birth. Every time I approached France, I burnt myself and quickly ran away—only to return, to burn myself again, and hurry away again, in an incessant coming and going around my cruel sun. I was a tether ball. Every stroke of the paddle hurt. After Entebbe, I finally understood and stopped my vibrating movement. The elastic had snapped.

After Entebbe, Marie-France burst into tears in my arms. She no longer wanted a divorce. Those whom life has separated, death or the threat of death can unite. I was once again her little hero: once again, and for a while, she could admire me. Nevertheless, I insisted on divorce: we could always live in sin afterward. Hand in hand, we appeared before the judge who separated us, and then went on a divorce trip. It was so much better than our honeymoon! How beautiful Honfleur was to the lovers! The prospect of a final separation had rekindled the flame of the lamp that had withstood so many storms; we still loved each other. Our love was smouldering, but it was under ashes.

How hard it is to have to be a hero every day to one's woman of all days! These women who can love only a victor, do they truly love? Of those who crowded into the Emperor's bed, how many sought to accompany or join him in his islands of defeat? To love a man is to love him vanquished too. I consumed the divorce in little sips, as though I wanted to prolong the pain. I suffer, therefore I am—that seemed to be my motto. I was too proud to beg for affection, too rational to want to conquer it again at sword's point, and perhaps too tired to be capable of it once more.

After Entebbe, the pain in my right hand lost its symbolic value, if not its mystery. It spread to my four limbs and from the periphery approached the center, making stops at my elbows and my knees. It took its time coming and going from one painful member to another, from one swollen finger to another, from one creaky morning to another clearer one, a rigor vitae that was gradually devouring me, a slow freeze. Every handshake was agony, every step an ordeal. My wanderer's feet, no longer capable of moving without painkillers, groaned under my weight. Numerous tests continued to indicate that I was in excellent health.

After Entebbe, my thoughts turned again to that father quickly classified as having "Died for France." For the first time I dared to admit that his death had not been *for* France but *by* France. Not by her alone, not by all of her, but by her just the same; for Vichy was also France, regardless of what the textbooks say. After Entebbe, I revived my father's name. Goldberg, father and son.

After Entebbe, the Vice-Minister of the Interior of an almost democratic Bolivian government discreetly let it be known that if France renewed her request for Barbie's extradition it would be given favorable consideration. But no sand should get into the gears of current negotiations. France, country of courtesy, did not want to be on bad terms with anyone. The Quai d'Orsay reopened the file very slowly, as though Barbie would live forever.

After Entebbe, I finally accepted the fact that I had been born twenty years too late. I would never be of the Glières.

I would never be a blood brother of the Resistance. Morette Cemetery would never be my resting place.

After Entebbe, I paid periodic visits to Surin Hershko, the Israeli soldier who had been wounded during the raid. For this knight of the doleful smile, heroism was not having volunteered for the mission during his last week of military service; it was not having vertebrae shattered by a bullet fired point blank by a Ugandan civilian whom he had just spared in compliance with orders; it was having to depend on someone day and night, for every movement and every need.

After Entebbe, I shaved off my ugly mustache. I didn't need it any longer; the orphan of old France had finished his mourning. I would go no more to La Paz to carry out the sentence of the Lyon court so that the France of Ramass would love me at last.

CHAPTER 11 *The Kill*

Work, Family, Country. Vichy's motto was not bad. I had already destroyed my family and settled accounts with my country. Only work remained. For so long I had been my work, belonging to the bank, serving it even when I criticized it, that I returned to my office with an almost physical pleasure such as good students feel on rediscovering the familiar smells and sights of school in September.

Many people called me, many invited me to lunch or dinner. They had seen me on television and undoubtedly thought I would still carry the strong scent of adventure. I buried myself in the files that had accumulated in my absence.

Today the Management Committee was to discuss a question that was in my bailiwick. In preparing my file for the meeting, I read over a paper dealing with another item on the agenda:

Confidential Memorandum

To: Members of the Management Committee
Department of General Accounting

From: The Chief Inspector of Branch Offices
Subject: Failure to comply with credit limits

On May 26, 1976, our attention was drawn to the fact that our Dijon branch had allowed a certain Nakache, a dealer in nonferrous metals, to overdraw his line of credit by two million francs. The branch director did not even consult with his area manager, for the alleged reason that the jew Nakache had said he was prepared to guarantee the loans with his personal assets. That was not done.

Nakache and Company has just obtained a declaration of bankruptcy.

A discreet inquiry by our auditing department has revealed that Nakache is a Hebrew well known for his shrewdness in business. Apart from the fact that this information should have been known to the branch director, it leaves us with little hope of recovering our loans. Nakache is currently unreachable at his residence or office, and his known assets in France turn out to be in the name of relatives or straw men.

I would not have brought these unfortunately rather common facts to the Committee's attention if I had not thought it in the interest of the Bank to make an example of a manager guilty of having so clearly exceeded his authority without any mitigating circumstances.

An indictment and a demand for sanctions followed.

I thought of computer statements summing up what are discreetly called "payment difficulties"; mentally I added a column: the Corsican Murracciole, the Alsatian Muller, the Pole Bilewski. And what epithet would one use for the Dupont? Heterosexual? I also noted that the memorandum observed the typographical code that deprives *Jew* of a capital letter.

The Nakache in question was surely guilty and the branch director an ass who deserved a thrashing. But that wasn't the problem. I tried to imagine what my colleagues' attitude would be when we reached this point on the agenda. I made a bet with myself that no one would react to the tone and terms of the Nakache memo.

Given my office, I plainly had nothing to say about this item on the agenda. Nevertheless, for once I followed the discussion with great interest. As it seemed more and more likely that I would win my bet, I asked myself whether I should intervene. Was it acceptable for someone to dare to express himself that way in writing a generation after Vichy in a company which was rather representative of the country's population, and for no one to protest? And above all, was it acceptable for me to remain silent? What did I have to complain about? A word which, after all, corresponded to reality, but the use of which betrayed the user's opinion. He was entitled to his opinion. But the fact that he expressed himself so naturally and in writing said a great deal about what he assumed to be his colleagues' opinion. So what was I doing in this fraternity?

Suddenly I decided to be courageous. It was not as spectacular as killing a Nazi, but isn't courage an everyday affair?—and besides, Barbie was still alive. I asked to speak:

"I do not have to take a position on the conclusions of the Nakache memo. Besides, I agree with them. But I would like to raise a point which seems to me of some interest, although I don't believe it would be useful to have it included in the minutes."

I motioned to the secretary who was recording the discussions; she looked at the president and then stopped.

I continued: "I am struck and, to be frank, shocked that the author of the memo believed that he should mention this not very commendable client's ethnic background. I would like him to tell us why."

Instantly a heavy silence descended around the large table. All eyes turned toward me, then slid sideways to the author of the memo, a lean, athletic man in spite of his approaching retirement. He was nonplussed.

"Isn't he Jewish?"

"Of course, but why mention it? He is also many other things!"

"Should I have written 'Mr.'?"

"If you had to use a term for him, why not 'the client' or 'a certain'?"

"That would be redundant. At any rate, it's not important."

"Then why did you repeat it? Is it because you see a link between his affiliation and the payment difficulty? Are we going to sort out clients as in the good old days?"

The president intervened: "This point, which is clearly outside the substance of the question at hand, reveals a stylistic slip rather than the author's true intentions. I thank Mr. Cojot, whom I am happy to welcome among us again, for calling attention to this detail. I suggest that Mr. Vérard retrieve all the copies of his memo, including the file copies, and circulate a modified version. I consider the incident closed."

The story went round the bank in half a day. Even an incident recorded in the minutes had never stirred up such a flurry. I received visits from union members, diehard secularists, Christian activists, and even a few Jews, all of whom, in one way or another, congratulated me.

During the entire week that followed, I remained astonished and relieved by my boldness. A few days later, the president called me on my direct line.

"Hello, Cojot? Are you free for lunch tomorrow? Forgive me for asking on such short notice, but I have wanted to invite you for a long time and I have just been informed of a change in my schedule."

"With pleasure, sir."

"Come by and pick me up at one o'clock. I'll take care of the reservations."

I put off the luncheon appointment I had for the next day. What the devil could the president want? I had hardly seen him since I returned from Latin America. I was so puzzled that on the morning of the next day I hesitated as to which tie to wear.

At one o'clock, I was ushered into the president's office.

"Come in," he said. "Sit down, I'll only be a minute."

He finished writing some paper or other. I remained standing in front of the bookcase, looking absent-mindedly at the superb bindings. Finally he came over to me, apparently pleased to see me, and led me to a small dining room: "I hope you will forgive me if we lunch at the bank, but I am expecting a call around two o'clock. . . . Ah! these time differences."

It was not one of those warriors' repasts that so many more or less senior executives tuck away in expense-account restaurants. No, everything was light: the wine, the artichoke hearts, the grillade vert-pré. Like the decor and the carpeting, the conversation was subdued.

"Cojot, I have wanted to see you for a long time, first of all to tell you how much we appreciate all you've done for us. And if I say 'we,' it is because I know that I reflect the opinion of your colleagues . . ."

"Thank you, sir, I have done my best. That is what I am paid for."

"I think I can speak of affection as well as esteem. . . . Even Vérard does not hold last week's incident against you. You should have heard them after we learned you were on that plane with your son!"

I had already realized that a pill which needed so heavy a coating of sugar had to be a bitter one.

"Cojot, for some time I have been thinking about your future and the best way to use your abilities. I must say that I am somewhat at a loss."

He did not seem to pay any attention to the food served by the waiter in white gloves; he picked at it distractedly, his hands fluttered, but he didn't leave anything.

"Considering your youth, your exceptional qualities," he continued, "I don't see very well how I can promote you without upsetting the rules of the bank and even of the profession.

"Since I am both judge and party, I will refrain for once from saying what I think of the rules governing banking careers. But you know my opinion about the profession's lemming-like behavior.

"Of course, you are one of those who by forcing . . . and even violating . . . the sometimes outmoded or timid rules of this profession have helped give our bank a clearer image than that of most others. Nevertheless, you know how delicate matters of personnel are."

"And of persons."

"Unquestionably. Even within the bank there would be no lack of people to protest a promotion that was too rapid. It would be a precedent with a high risk of inflation."

"Sir, do you think I should look for another position?"

He put his glass down lightly without even indulging in the farce of a raised eyebrow, though perhaps a little surprised to have come to the main course so quickly.

"That would be unfortunate for the bank, Cojot, and I would be very sorry personally . . . but just between us, and from your point of view, I must say that I would understand perfectly . . . deep down, I would even approve, and if I were your age, I would envy you."

"Are you encouraging me?"

"As president, certainly not. As a friend, I see the pros and cons. What are you going to do with all the good years ahead of you, the prime of your life . . . champ at the bit? Should you ask for my help I can't give it to you officially, of course, but I will have a well-placed friend assist you instead. He will have more leeway."

"And if I decide to stay?"

"Then of course we would offer you something—overseas, for instance, but you have just come back, or some interesting subsidiary."

"Exile, so to speak. What about my present position?"

He motioned to the waiter to serve the coffee.

"That is one of the subjects I wanted to speak to you about. You yourself have pointed out on many occasions how illogical and costly it is to maintain research services as dispersed as ours. We would like to group them together. No one doubts that you would be the most qualified person to take charge of the combined department. But you are familiar with the Legendre problem, aren't you? What can I do with a fifty-three-year-old man of his rank? If you would agree to be his second in command—that is to say, the first in fact—that would be a solution. . . . Here, take my cigar-cutter. . . . In this profession it is a real tragedy to succeed too quickly. I wonder what we will do with all those brilliant students we hired during the period of euphoria when they reach forty. We will have to sharpen the tip of the hierarchical pyramid again."

"It will become an obelisk!"

"Quite so."

"Or people must be encouraged to leave."

"It's always the best ones who go."

Suddenly this conversation ceased to interest me.

"In short, you are advising me to leave?"

"It is not in the bank's interests," he said with a sorrowfully sincere expression, "but it is in yours. I would not advise you to go against your own best interests."

The white-gloved waiter appeared suddenly with an empty tray.

"A call from New York, sir. Will you take it here?"

While the president gathered his recollections of English I looked around the Directoire dining room and already felt out of it. Curiously enough, I was rather relieved to be pushed out in this way. Regardless of what the labor agreement says, I was being persuaded to resign, and if I wanted to save face, it would cost me the golden handshake that is given instead of severance pay in these professions of guaranteed employment.

I realized that since childhood I had been leading the life of a schizophrenic. Two individuals cohabited within the same skin, and not always peacefully. As time went on this split was less and less tolerable. I would have to restore my unity or break in two irreparably. The president's decision told me that the moment had come, the moment of truth for Michel Cojot, banker. "A las cinco de la tarde . . . ," the beginnning of the end.

"Well, my dear Cojot, where are you in your thinking?"

He was back from New York.

"Pardon me if I seem to change the subject. Have you had any reactions to my remarks at the last Management Committee meeting?"

The president's face and even his voice hardened almost imperceptibly: "Cojot, everyone here has known for a long time that you are Jewish, and if that bothers anyone I am unaware of it. You, perhaps? . . . I imagine that this bank has the usual share of imbeciles, perhaps a few more given the sociology of the profession, but they have enough good sense to keep their opinions to themselves, apart from an occasional slip of the pen. . . . In any case, I can assure you that neither this incident nor your affiliation has ever carried any weight in my mind or in the judgments passed on you during your brilliant career.

"You are an *écorché*, Cojot, a man with an overly thin skin. That undoubtedly makes you more intelligent, but also more sensitive, too sensitive. Let's admit that Vérard revealed his true feelings in his unfortunate memo. What do you want to do about it? Redirect his conscience? Punish him for an opinion? Kill him? That seems to me to be neither very convenient nor in the Jewish tradition. By wanting everyone to love you you are going to make everyone detest you. You cannot force hearts. Be satisfied with respect, that is already a great deal."

"Sir, I have decided to leave."

"You can see that I regret it very much but, as I told you, I understand and I will help you indirectly, should a man of your talent need help."

There was a brief silence filled with sips of coffee.

"Sir, this is probably one of our last private conversations. I would like to ask you a personal question that has nothing to do with what we've talked about so far."

He motioned to me to continue.

"Sir, do you believe in what you are doing?"

The president was a little surprised. I continued.

"In particular, did you believe in what you did when, contrary to our studies, you almost automatically approved all requests to open more branches, causing the inflation of personnel which today presents you with so many problems?"

To give himself time to reflect, the president took a double Punch Corona, cut off its head, and lit it according to the rules.

"What a strange question. You're telling me that, of your own free will, you will soon be looking for another position; I tell you that I'm perfectly willing to help you, and instead of speaking to me about your future, you subject me to an examination of conscience. But I won't shy away from it."

He paused again briefly.

"Admittedly, to preside over this bank or any other is not the fulfillment of my childhood ambition—I wanted to be a painter—or even of my adolescent dreams. But exciting jobs are rare in this century, when most of the great reasons for living have been reasons for dying. I served the State for a few years with no illusions and I served it again by leaving it.

"Since I was lucky enough to belong to one of the first families of the Republic, it was assumed that I was capable of running a large enterprise. I understand how discouraging this method of appointment can be for those who have spent their lives working their way up the ladder. Still, the aristocracy of competitive examinations is somewhat less unfair than the aristocracy of birth or wealth, and I don't believe that I have discharged my responsibilities any less well than my predecessors. Since I do not have much personal wealth—nor do you, I believe—I have to work to support my family; and I don't see why I should spit in my soup."

The president took a long draw on his cigar, so useful for seeking inspiration. He continued: "I know that you were very critical of the expenses incurred during the race for branches, which you considered ill-advised. This may come as a surprise to you, but of everything I have done here, that is perhaps what I believe in most.

"If our regulatory authorities have for so long endorsed a system that encourages us to expand at will, I must assume that they are getting something out of it. I am neither Governor of the Bank of France nor Minister of Finance. I am content to try to run this bank in its own best interests, which is not an easy task in itself. It is not up to me or to any other private person to assess the common interest. But it was undoubtedly less costly to the country for banks to keep the young unemployed warm—giving them a chance to rise in addition—than to pay the riot troops to keep them from throwing cobblestones.

"Remember the great fear of May '68, which just about coincided with the beginning of this expansion policy. The banks have been the fire-wall of another May '68. We are troops of the counterrevolution, Cojot, with this major difference: we haven't shot anyone. Only the young unemployed are desperate enough for revolution. The unions preaching both employment and revolution are applying the brake and the accelerator at the same time. All things considered, they, too, are counterrevolutionaries, but they don't know it. To avoid another May '68, or worse, isn't it worth a few too many branches? If Léon Blum had taken a couple of divisions to the Rhine when there was still time, what calamities wouldn't he have spared us! And what criticism he would have brought upon himself! Sometimes I tell myself that I have been more useful to the State here than when I was in government service.

"Moreover, to return to the matter of this House, nothing says that the present state of affairs will continue forever. Remember the crash of the Banque Nationale de Crédit, remember your analyses. The May '68 generation is getting middle-aged and its successors seem to prefer the charms of nature to those of the cobblestones. When we are finally asked to slow down, I hope to make my stand in a strong position.

"Cojot, this is a game with rules that I didn't make. If one wants to play, one must follow the rules. I try to play my role. I am not so power-hungry that this gives me a reason for living. If our world is in such a sorry state, it is in large measure because the method by which its leaders are recruited tends to select those who have an unhealthy appetite for power. They make excellent subordinates but abominable leaders who would not hesitate to massacre their own to satisfy their neurosis. Cojot, I am trying to do what I have to do, conscientiously but without passion, and I feel it's better that way. I don't want to be a crusader without a crusade. When I have enough of balance sheets and bowing and scraping, I think of my children's smiles and I take refuge at home, at Pont-Audemer, among peasants who are quite happy to produce milk that no one knows what to do with."

After this rare interlude of candor, the president once more donned his mask. Had he ever removed it?

After a few innocuous remarks he rose from his chair. We left the dining room together. We stopped in front of the door to his office. Smiling like a hostess thanking her guests for having come, he said: "Have you any idea of the date when you . . . you might leave? Take all the time you need, but let me know as soon as you have decided. Why don't you send me a little letter. As you know, I would like to take that opportunity to make a few changes in our organization chart. . . . Goodbye, Cojot, good luck."

The door closed. I was alone like a little boy outside the teacher's room.

CHAPTER 12 *Burial of My Father*

Only after I had left my wife and my bank was I able to understand the obvious: the void that I had always tried to lean on, that was my father, so absent, so abstract, so powerful, immortal, immense, insurmountable. In scaling the Alps of generations I had to ascend, without a guide, a peak that was inaccessible because it was nonexistent. It was this void which had led me to climb the Andes, to drive myself harder and harder, to seek out men who would protect or admire me. All in vain. Grandfathers and uncles had disappeared into the dark sky, and I couldn't spend my life looking for a shadow where there had never been one: a friend, a boss, a status, an idea—these are not, nor would they ever become, my father.

I decided to find him, for his sake but much more for mine. I wanted to demythify him, to humanize him and bring him down to my level, in order eventually to surpass him. Perhaps I also wanted his forgiveness for having stolen his woman from him once upon a time.

The natural starting place for such a voyage was my mother. She helped me, but she had forgotten so much and

179

so distorted reality. Over the years she had ascribed so many virtues to her first husband that he seemed scarcely human. If I insisted on finding a flaw it became a virtue. For quick-tempered she would say energetic, for tactless she would say frank, for short she would say husky.

She had discarded his letters, which would have been just so many documents likely to send us to the oven. She had destroyed every trace of him, except me. And it was up to me to unravel the tangled skeins of memory. So I returned to the places that had mattered to him and found people to whom he had mattered.

Beaune-la-Rolande. For me this name flags a time when the secondary meaning of words had become the main one: like *être arrêté*—"to be stopped, to be arrested," or *monter au front*—"to go to the front of the room, to go to the firing-line." Beaunelarolande, which I learned before I knew how to read, continued to sound strange. Beaune l'Arolande, with its *a* depriving of freedom, as "amoral" is deprived of morality. La Rolande, wife of Roland the Valiant. La Rolande, Blackie, the family cows. I was just as surprised to learn that it was also the name of a peaceful little town of the Gâtinais as I had been to learn that the maquis was also a kind of shrubbery or that one could also denounce a contract.

Beaune-la-Rolande: 4, 4 km. The signpost was no different from others bearing equally earthy names: le Pavé-de-Juranville, Foncerive, Bréfontaine, Saint-Loup-des-Vignes. There was no hint that for thousands of men, women, and children Beaune had served as the depot of death. La Rolande, which flows to the Loing and to distant parts.

I went to the city hall. "Which camp was your father in?" they asked me. "The prisoners' camp or . . . the other?"

The other, the unspeakable.

At the site of the camp a school had been built where children laughed, children like those who were separated from their mothers one evil day and whose cries the old people still hear.

The camp's yellowed and crumpled records were made available to me. With the usual upstrokes and down-strokes, they recorded the condition of the supplies and the quarters, the escapes and the medical discharges. I imagined the customs officers, with their southern accents, running the camp, satisfying their superiors and their consciences at the same time by cultivating the nonchalance so widely attributed to them. In the beginning they were only moderately vigilant, thus permitting a good number of escapes.

I found a trace of my father in the infirmary records among detainees who were sick, looking for a dispensation of something or just for a warm place to spend the morning. On the other hand, his name did not appear on the list of the thirty-five prisoners released on September 13— thirty-four sick persons and one non-Jew.

Touching these papers—so ordinary, so familiar— gave me the strange feeling that I was going back in time, trivializing history. The directive on the cleanliness of the quarters resembled those of my days in the service so much that you could hardly tell them apart: same format, same style, same heading, same care in underlining prettily. I could have been as well the author as the subject of the order. I, too, have worn the uniform of an army that looked with suspicion on persons whose features were different from theirs.

There, too, it will take thirty years for the sons to utter the father's cry. One day French literature will be enriched by a book written by the son of a harki.* To those who will express surprise that he has waited so long, he and his brothers will reply: "Before we did not dare remember and had not yet found a voice."

I discovered a muddy photograph of a bureaucratic outdoor activity. The military uniforms have remained virtually unchanged since then: only the civilian clothes are dated. It is probably the arrival, the reception; some men are still wearing ties and have creases in their trousers. The one who is "coming up" is so bold as to put his two hands on the little table. They are still among human beings, among Frenchmen. In the good care of Captain Cucuat. I scanned the photograph the way a person with a rendezvous scans a crowd. There in the first row, who is that detainee whose hairline is like mine, whose lips are

*The harkis were Algerians who served voluntarily in the French army during the Algerian War. After independence, a number of them were resettled in France. Their French-born children, who are ethnically Arabs, legally French, generally Moslem, are often despised in France as Arabs and in Algeria as the offspring of traitors.

fleshy like mine? He keeps his hands in front of him, he is waiting. Could he be my father, the infantryman Joseph Goldberg, the holder of the Croix de Guerre with Bronze Star? The photo was mute, but I wanted so much to believe.

The Gâtinais was sad for my lonely pilgrimage, the weather typical of All Saints' Day—cold and misty. A low sky, pierced here and there by a steeple, hung over the gloomy plain. I was in France's heart, in eternal France, the France of no trespassing, of family plots and rural cops à la Stan Laurel, where fatherland and hometown converge, where the French Krauts, the "Boches du Nord," fleeing the German armies of May-June 1940, were penned in.

The town's war-dead monument is in the center of Beaune-la-Rolande and is made of local stone. The monument to the Jews is on the outskirts, of black marble from afar covered with unpronounceable names. At the time of the Occupation, the town counted one Jewish family among its residents: they were eventually denounced, and mother and one daughter were caught. Probably out of shame, they were not sent to the local camp but to the one in Pithiviers, 18 km away, before they disappeared to the east. Their names are not inscribed on the monument to the town's war dead.

I met Maurice, a survivor of Auschwitz, near the Bastille. He had known my father before the war and had met him again in the camp. A Polish Jew from Belleville, speaking fluent cockney-French, at the age of sixty-five he was still a powerful figure of a man. Arrested because he was a resister, a Jew, and a Communist, he had compounded grounds for deportation, and the number tattooed on his forearm was both his identity card and his decoration. He had returned from Upper Silesia strengthened, ennobled, redeemed.

"In Auschwitz," he said, "your father told me that he had ten chances to escape from Beaune-la-Rolande. . . . But he didn't want to leave the others, he said. He wanted to help them. How stupid! And besides, he didn't think it would be so terrible. . . . I told him: 'They can't kill us all. Some of us are bound to come through, and I'll be among them.' At the time, I was a member of the Central Committee of Communist Youth, and the Party saved me."

"How?"

"One day I left the mine where I was working ten minutes early. I had misjudged the time. I was in for fifty truncheon blows on the right hand. I had said that I was right-handed though actually I'm left-handed. If you withdrew your hand you got a bullet in the back of the neck. I lost three fingers there, see? But I didn't withdraw my hand. So afterward, the SS shook my other hand and said: 'At least you are a sport!'

"All the same I had seven boils, and the infection was spreading. Fortunately, I was recognized by a Party comrade—still a great guy, even though I no longer always agree with him. He saw my condition.

" 'You won't pull through, you need a scam. You're going to do us and yourself a favor at the same time.' They used pieces of iron and a bicycle inner tube to draw out the pus and had me assigned to the kitchens on condition that I arrange to steal forty liters of soup every day, the good SS soup, for sick Party members. 'And what about the others?' I asked. 'Don't worry about the others. It is better for us to survive than for everyone to die off.' I gave a little soup to my pals too, but in the camp you had to think of yourself first. If you wanted to survive you had to be a bit of a bastard."

"And my father?"

"After surviving a year in Auschwitz, which took some doing, your father no longer had the will to live. He was a good guy, but he thought too much, he was too human. And besides, he didn't weigh much, no more than a hundred pounds when I last saw him. He couldn't believe that a civilization could sink so low and that the world would let it happen. . . . Once, it was a Sunday morning, we heard Allied planes and there was an alert. We all hoped they were going to bomb the gas chambers, the railway, the SS buildings, that it was all for us. . . . Fat chance! They were trying to hit the synthetic rubber plant. The only bomb that fell on the camp was a mistake. For your father, it was as if he had received a fist in his face. And he wasn't the only one. . . . He died because he no longer had the will to hold on. . . ."

"In spite of us?"

"Well, yes. He loved you, you and your mother. He

spoke of you often, but that wasn't enough to keep him alive."

Maurice thought for a moment, his mind no doubt crowded with memories.

"All the same, he found himself a pretty cushy job. He was inside most of the time. He cleaned a cell block. It wasn't too hard and, above all, it wasn't outdoors."

"Do you know how he died?"

"After a while, it must have been the end of '44, I didn't see him any more. It wasn't easy for us to see each other. We were not in the same group. He must have died of exhaustion, a 'Moslem,' as we called the zombies who dragged themselves around with empty eyes and no longer cared, or he was gassed, which amounts to the same thing. . . . It's a pity, he must have died just before the liberation of the camp in January '45."

So in two hours, over a 3,50 franc coffee, I learned that my father had not been a hero, that he had not spit in his torturers' faces before dying, that he had not dug a tunnel, that he had not made a dagger out of his tin plate, that he had not been hung as an example, that he had not thrown himself against the electrified barbed wire. And yet I was satisfied, satisfied to know Maurice, to know that he respected my father, and especially, that he had made him a little more real for me.

I could not help smiling as I ascended the endlessly winding stairs. What would be the look on the face of this grandmother whom I was visiting to talk about a man who had been her lover more than forty years earlier?

She had a beautiful head of gray hair and she remembered. She had loved him, therefore he was still alive, she gave him substance. She gazed at me affectionately, for I too revived a ghost for her. She said I resembled him at the age when they had known each other.

For a long time she spoke softly of him, of herself, of everything and of nothing. She spoke to me as she would have to the son I might have been. I left her without having learned anything essential, and yet I was happy, satisfied as after making love. By recalling how he had eaten his first oysters, how badly he danced, how he liked flowers and Léon Blum and latkes and France, she had made my father human.

I went to Charbonnières-les-Bains, the place of my last common memory with him. Everything had given way to a building without a past. In Lyon itself, in an alleyway that linked the Place des Terreaux with the rue Ste. Catherine, I went to the last stairway he had ascended as a free man. The French Militia was waiting for him on the third floor. Behind the glass door, a secretary was typing and drinking coffee. I left, breathing deeply as I had on the steps of the Daiquiri, and relieved. I looked around me. Lyon was also a beautiful city, in spite of those crows whose flight weighed so heavy in my memory.

I also went to Précy-sous-Thil, a little village in the

Côte d'Or, where we had been made welcome.

Behind the door a voice trembled: "Who is it?"

"Is Mme. Voye here?"

The door creaked open, revealing an old woman in black and white like so many we grow in the country. She looked at me with the apprehension of women always prepared for bad news.

"Do you remember the little boy who used to spend hours in your candy store during the war?"

"Little Jean Collenot? I should hope so!"

"I am he."

"Impossible! Come in . . . and bring your little girl. . . . Come in."

She immediately offered Aviva some sweets: "Here, have some candy . . . like your father when he was your age. . . ."

"My father doesn't want me to, he says it causes cavities."

"Just this once, he won't say anything!"

I asked her if she remembered my father.

"Of course I remember him."

"Then would you be kind enough to talk to me about him?"

She too spoke of him as though he were alive; she said that he was always ready to be helpful—and she added that some people in the village were sure he was a Jew: "I don't know anything about it. Was it true?"

Not daring to embrace me as tightly as she would have liked, she made up for it with my daughter.

Surely the portrait of my father remained incomplete, but he was no longer the hero with the empty eyesockets of a Greek god that my imagination had created. Human again, he was also mortal again. I was finally able to begin laying him—and myself—to rest.

EPILOGUE *The Fortieth Year*

Thus, the important things I learned in forty years take fewer than two hundred pages to tell. Was so much suffering necessary to discover these obvious facts?

Hardly were they down on paper when the portraits rose up and ran away. My pen-scalpel emphasized this or that trait, forgot the rounded line, let itself be word-pecked, excised the wart, and omitted the smile in the corner of the eye. Cruelty of an apprentice-author, vanity of a man beseeching denials. Anxiety of the man unshielded, naked, who does not know whether his readers will seize the opportunity to embrace him, to hurt him, or to ignore him. Will writing extinguish the pain in this right hand which has not killed? Will writing help me to be reborn, or did I shoot a book through my head?

Beyond the vicissitudes of every life, the story is banal. It is the story of a child who did not want to grow old without burying papa; the story of a Jew with a possessive mother—forgive the redundancy; the story of a boy who wanted so much to be like the others as a kid but couldn't bear it as an adult; the story of a good student who believed that school would last forever; the story of a Parisian who thought that his taste for *soupe à l'oignon* rooted him in the French soil as well; the story of a father who adored his sons but abandoned his foolish reserve only with his daughter; the story of a man who hated himself so much that he did not believe a good woman could love him; the story of a husband who drove his blonde to lie by another who will also be forty one morning; the story of a Frenchman who believed that Marianne, symbol of the Republic, was made of flesh and wanted her to love him above others; the story of a Jew who believed that Israel was waiting for him; the story of a French Jew who had to come all the way to America to feel truly French; the story of a banker who did not believe in money; the story of one three-billionth of humanity who looked for Meaning in his own existence; the story of an atom that could no longer bear to be split; the story of a mortal who thought he could defy life; the story of a Scorpio who tried to rise from his ashes.

What will remain of all this in thirty years? Who still remembers Schwartzbard, who killed Petlioura, a great pogrom-maker, in a Paris street between the two wars? Who remembers Franckforter, who killed the head of the Swiss Nazi party in Davos before the war after the war to end all wars? What will be left of my story the day after tomorrow? Three adults—my children—struggling in their turn against the fortieth year and a book sold at a discount, three for twelve francs, in a sidewalk stall.

To act so as to be—illusion; to kill to be—madness; to have so as to be—absurdity. To love in order to be—the essential in one short phrase. All the rest is literature.